Antony Francis Campbell SJ

'Go Think'

InterfaceTheology:
Incorporating *Sapientia et Sciencia* and in association with *Wort und Antwort* (Germany)
Volume 7, Number 1, 2021

Subscription rates
Print Local: Individual Aus $55, Institutions Aus $65.
Overseas: Individuals US $60, Institutions US $65.

Interface Theology is a biannual refereed journal of theology published in print, Epub and PDF by ATF Press Publishing Group.
The journal is a scholarly ecumenical and interdisciplinary publication, aiming to serve the church and its mission, promoting a broad-based interpretation of Christian theology within a trinitarian context, encouraging dialogue between Christianity and other faiths, and exploring the interface between faith and culture. It is published in English for an international audience.

ISSN 2203-465X
Cover art work Yvonne Ashby

ISBN: 978-1-922737-21-2   soft
        978-1-922737-22-9   hard
        978-1-922737-23-6   epub
        978-1-922737-24-3   pdf

THEOLOGY

An imprint of ATF Theology part of the ATF Press Publishing Group which is owned by
ATF (Australia) Ltd.
PO Box 234,
Brompton, SA, 5007
Australia
www.atfpress.com
Making a lasting impact

Antony Francis Campbell SJ

'Go Think'

THEOLOGY
2021

Table of Contents

InterfaceTheology 7/1 2021

Editorial

'Go, think' was the mantra used in his life, in his dealings with students and in some of the written Work by Antony (Tony) Francis Campbell, SJ.

A New Zealander by birth, a Jesuit by choice Tony studied and taught in a variety of places around the world but lived and taught for much of his life in Australia, far from the centre of the academic work that he loved and breathed, was an author of many books including a number with ATF Press.

This edition of Interface Theology is devoted to the life and work of Tony Campbell and has contributions by close colleagues and friends, members of the Australian Jesuit community and those who were his friends and colleagues outside of the Jesuits.

I first came to know Tony through his collaboration with the Mark O'Brien, OP. I met him on a number of occasions socially with Mark and then as his publisher through ATF Press. He gave the Press the honour of publishing a number of books with him. It indeed was an honour for us as Tony had previously published with some of the larger well known US based academic publishers. Working with Tony led also to a strong personal friendship and we would spend many times on the phone or in person talking about the world, the Catholic Church and publishing, at times sparring and other times agreeing. These times were always one I cherished and enjoyed. He had an innate understanding of publishing from his many years of working with publishers but a strong belief and appreciation of the importance of the work of ATF Press. For this, and for the many kindnesses I received from him, I will always have a great admiratio and respect him for him as a scholar, colleague and friend

It is once again an honour and a privilege to publish this collection of essays in honour of Tony with the hope the volume captures the essence of the man, scholar, teacher and writer.

Hilary Dominic Regan
October 2021

L'Chaim!

Nicole Rotaru, RSM

It is good that we can come together to honour and celebrate the incredibly rich life of Antony Francis Campbell—a staunchly loyal Jesuit who acknowledged the strengths and vulnerabilities of the Society and firmly planted his feet in Jesuit earth.

My deepest sympathy to every Jesuit. In your own unique ways you influenced Tony and shared with him the Ignatian charism and Jesuit life. My deepest sympathy to everyone else who knew Tony, colleagues, students and friends. I am especially mindful of long term friends. You, too, were part of his vibrant life.

I feel very honoured and privileged Brian, that you asked me to share some reflections about Tony. Thank you. We all come with our own experiences of this man. May our gathering enable us all to know deepening solace, wonder and gratitude.

> When I consider your vastness, O God,
> what are we that we are so special to you?
> Yet we are![1]
>
> Psalm 8:3–6

Like the Psalmist, Tony tussled with this too. He marvelled much about the awesomeness, the bigness of God caring for him, caring for us all. His wondering came up in various ways. He often referred to conversations with his friend Paddy Meagher. Did Paddy believe in an unconditionally loving God given all the struggles and heartbreaking situations he had encountered in his missionary work? Paddy's thoughtful pause ended with a definite 'Yes!'

---

1. This was Tony's translation of Ps 8: 3–6. See Frank Gill, *Have Life More Abundantly* Adelaide: (ATF Press, 2013), 22.

Tony often puzzled over God's unconditional love and how that fitted with the mess we have made of much of our world and the violent injustices.

For a long time he also wanted to know if God really existed. Ironically, there was a period in his life as a Jesuit where he took on an atheist's stance. I remember him telling me that sometime before taking solemn vows he realised, 'Hell, I'm jealously in love with God.' Tony believed, believed deeply. He just wanted to know.

Antony Francis Campbell once described himself as 'a New Zealander by birth, an Australian Jesuit by choice and a lover of the Older Testament by passion.'

Family

Nancy, an accomplished pianist, loving wife and dedicated mother and Bill, a quiet, resourceful and successful manager of a meat factory were Tony's parents. His brothers John, Henry and Jeremy completed the Campbell household along with Monty, the dog. Tony often described childhood as care-free. He spent much of his free time roaming along the banks of the river at the edge of their family property in New Zealand with his best mate, Mike, and their eyes keenly peeled for rabbits to take a shot at.

After school he often went to his dad's office and waited to catch a ride home. Once out of town, Tony took over the wheel under the watchful eye of his dad as they chatted about the day.

At home he often watched his mum tending Jeremy who had been diagnosed with autism. Tony often said that part of his faith was shaped by the fact that Jeremy was not cured of autism when he was taken to Lourdes by his mum. When Jeremy became agitated, mother often called on Tony to calm him.

Henry was a great pianist, following in the footsteps of his mother. Visits to see Henry in London, where he had made his home, were not easy, though there were moments of Tony hearing his brother's brilliance as he played Chopin, Shubert and Joplin.

In Tony's eyes, John would probably have been a brilliant lawyer or stockbroker, had he not died in a plane accident while serving in the air force. In 1953 Tony joined the Jesuits. They were the best, he said.

Parkville

After studies at Loyola College, Watsonia, Melbourne University, Lyon-Fouviere, the Pontifical Biblical Institute in Rome and time in London, Israel and Munich and finally doctoral studies at the then Claremont Graduate School in California, Tony settled into Jesuit Theological College, Parkville. He took on a range of roles: administration, teaching, research and writing and supervising doctoral students.

Tony was a formidable, creative administrator as dean of studies and later principal. He was instrumental in transforming theological studies and ensuring that the new venture of an ecumenical theologate, United Faculty of Theology (UFT), thrived.

Much of Tony's research and writing was done late at night into the early morning. He was an erudite scholar steeped in integrity. He writes in *Ancient Bible: Modern Faith*: 'The passion for integrity and the making of meaning fuels much of my faith and biblical interpretation.'[2]

First proofs, August 4, 2009, *Ancient Bible: Modern Faith*, p. 8

His classes at UFT and no doubt those in Berkeley California were almost indescribable. Certainly not point by point. Tangents, ideas, links with the current religious, social and political positions sprang up everywhere. He was at once, all over the place, inspiring, paradoxical, challenging, engaging and even a tad crazy. He stretched minds, expanded hearts and fired spirits.

For years on Thursday afternoons into the wee hours of Friday morning Mark O'Brien and Tony Campbell plumbed and mulled over texts and wrote several books together, aided by the best Scotch. Two magnificent men, a Dominican and a Jesuit, who enjoyed one another's company, respected each other's intellect and capacity for rigorous attention to the text. Beyond their writing and research they met regularly at Papa Gino's in Lygon Street to share a pizza, red wine and plenty of gossip and conversation sorting out the world.

Tony was an intuitive, compassionate spiritual director. He could be with you in those tough places of vulnerability, shame and regret and leave you with a feeling of ease and hope.

---

2. First proofs, August 4, 2009, *Ancient Bible: Modern Faith,* p. 8

Sabbaticals

Tony did his doctoral studies at the Claremont Graduate School, California. Our Lady of the Assumption Catholic Church, Claremont became his primary base. He made many good friends and was greatly appreciated and valued for his parish involvements.

During this time, he met Feliz Gil-Jimenez, a Felician Sister. Feliz was a dynamic teacher at OLA School for many years and later became the Principal. Her energies extended to OLA Parish where she was involved in many activities. Tony and Feliz became long and lasting friends. Their abiding friendship of forty-seven years was nourished by letters and phone calls.

In *God First Loved Us*, Tony wrote:

> The incarnation is the unique and unsurpassable expression of God's love for us'.[3]

> For me, this describes Tony's love for Feliz and Feliz's love for Tony.

Sabbaticals were also a concentrated time for further research and writing. Tony's contributions to scholarship are vast. A look at the Jesuit website will leave you in sheer admiration.

Tony's writings on Samuel have been particularly significant. *The Ark Narrative*, Commentaries on both 1 and 2 Samuel, and it is said, that his work in, *Of Prophets and Kings: A Late Ninth-Century Document contains* the most comprehensive examination so far of Pre-Deuteronomistic composition in Samuel and Kings.

Just days ago, Mark O'Brien gave Tony the good news that his writing on 2 Samuel for the New Jerome Biblical Commentary was done and dusted.

Tony immersed himself in the texts to the point of saturation. The texts fascinated him, drawing him into ever deepening and expanding levels of possible understanding. I say possible, as Tony had the deepest reverence and respect for the text. Mystery was there! What was its message? Its many and varied messages?

---

3. AF Campbell, 2002, *god First Loved Us*: The challenge of Accepting Unconditional love (new york: Paulist Press, 2000), 53.

The text was alive for Tony. He was a passionate scholar and delighted in sharing his passion with others. There were many times when I would say, 'Tony, it's OK to take a breath here, a full stop.'

Tony would mull for days on end to find the most appropriate word to convey what he wanted to say. I remember vividly several of our long walks at Warrandyte where he listed umpteen words to capture the title of the work he and Mark were doing on the Deuteronomistic History. Finally, he settled on *Unfolding. Unfolding the Deuteronomistic History.*

When Tony reached seventy-five years he asked the Council of Jesuit Theological College (JTC) for Emeritus status and retirement from JTC and UFT. He was presented with a testimonial document—part of it said, 'His teaching has combined evocation and provocation in the best sense of those terms. He has mentored research students with scholarly exactitude and personal care. He has published books of the highest scholarly quality, of engaging readability, and of passionate conviction.'

Campion

The move from Parkville to Campion was not an easy transition for Tony. He missed the academic-student environment, the free ranging conversations, the spacious back garden and glorious trees, the easy access to the UFT Library. And more Lygon Street, where Tony met with dear friends Bill Uren, Peter Steele and Michael Stoney and many other Jesuits, as well as many other friends.

A change of study rooms reveals the stark enormity of the transition. Tony's study in Parkville had a ceiling to floor bookcase, numerous filing cabinets and stacks and piles of books and papers on the floor and even the arm chair. His Campion room had a small book case of selected texts and one filing cabinet. What remained the same were the numerous piles of paper scattered around.

Gradually Tony came to enjoy his Campion room. The outlook to the garden, the trees and the sound of the birds were a delight. More, he grew in appreciation of the evening gathering with the community, enjoying a drink in the sitting room before dinner and those spontaneous, one to one conversations.

Faith was a recurring part of our conversations and became even more so during his time at Campion. Tony's faith was always firmly grounded in integrity.

For him, Scripture was there for us to 'Go think!' Scripture 'invites to thought, rather than imposes it'. For Tony, the diverse and contrary positions in scripture had 'the indispensable role of arousing feeling, firing imagination, and fuelling faith'.[4]

As the months and years passed at Campion, Tony slowly started to come to grips with the challenges of being diagnosed with Binswanger's disease, a subcortical vascular dementia. Tony was confronted with his slow and unsteady gait, frequent falls and some short term forgetfulness. Campion Community and the staff supported him lovingly through these changes. Their time, patience and care meant a lot to him. As the symptoms became increasingly more debilitating, it was clear that Tony needed more fulltime intensive care. Thus, his eventual move to Nazareth House after several hospital stays and a long spell in St George's Rehab, Kew.

Nazareth House

For the first few months at Nazareth House Tony was in Holy Family Wing. His small single bedroom housed a desk, computer and a handful of books. While there, he still went for coffee to a couple of cafes nearby and a few times managed a meal out. But that time was short.

On a Sunday, after sharing lunch in the dining room with the other residents, Tony was making his way back to his room using the walker. Suddenly his legs stopped walking. That shift necessitated moving Tony to a shared room in St Joseph's Wing, where the staff could provide the extra care he needed.

On a few occasions it was possible to take Tony in a wheel chair to the balcony or into the garden. He enjoyed the changing skies, the fresh breeze, trees and birds. These little outings did not last. Sitting in a wheel chair became too hard. Tony was confined to bed.

While constant adjustments had to be made by Tony and the staff, a strong bond of respect, gratitude and affection developed. He knew

---

4. AF Campbell and MA O'Brien, 2000, *Unfolding the Deuteronomistic History: Origins, Upgrades, Present Text* (Minneapolis: Fortress Press, 2000), 7

many of the carers by name; where they originated from—Uganda, India, Philippines, Italy, Ireland, Hungary and Australia; and who had children.

Not long ago, while sitting on Tony's bed I said, 'Tony you are doing a Job. You taught Job many times at UFT, now you are surely living the experience.' He grinned broadly, paused, and replied:

> I can't eat and drink.
> I can't read and write.
> I can't walk and talk.

And in the last days, Tony Campbell, wordsmith par excellence moved into mouthing one word at a time in a bare whisper. And then no words came.

In all this bodily diminishment, I have been constantly in awe at Tony's humility and patience. He didn't quite agree about being humble and patient, but he was. And he was gracious and grateful. For months Tony had to be fed, to be constantly repositioned in bed, to be toileted, to be washed. He could do none of these things for himself. The man who was larger than life, who made his presence felt whenever he strode into a room became totally dependent in having his bodily needs met.

Yes, Tony got frustrated and angry, and confusion played havoc with his state of being, till things were sorted out. But, by and large, his attitude was gracious and grateful. His intellect remained fairly astute and keen and his affections loving and loyal.

My friendship with Tony Campbell spans forty-one years. He has been teacher, spiritual director, workshop colleague and deeply loving faithful friend. I've known his wacky, quirky nonsense, infuriating larrikin, prattle side and his deep compassion. Sometimes, he was an absolute conundrum and utterly impossible. We enjoyed countless picnics, walks by rivers and along bush tracks, movies, hours of listening to music and a tender comfortability being together in silence.

Tony believed God to be unconditionally loving and committed to us. In his final days, I felt his disposition was reflected in his words from *The Whisper of Spirit*, 'The goal of the journey: fuller awareness of the feeling for our restlessness, in search of the rest, that is the source of the existence of the universe.'[5]

---

5. AF Campbell, *The Whisper of Spirit*: A Believable god grand Rapids: Eerdmans, 2008), xiii

I believe that you, Antony Francis Campbell, have seen with your own eyes and felt with your own heart the source of the existence of the universe whom you sought with the whole of you. When you died at 2.04 am on August 2, it was clear you finally knew. Your face, Tony, was utterly, utterly radiant.

Thank you, my dearest friend Tony, for your immense fearsome integrity, your profound loving fidelity. L'Chaim!

Nicole Rotaru RSM
6 August 2020

Fr Tony Campbell, SJ: A Obituary[1]

Brendan Byrne, SJ

Fr Tony Campbell SJ died on 2 August 2020, and was farewelled at a Funeral Mass on 6 August 2020.

Tony Campbell, a New Zealander by birth, was educated by the Marist Fathers at Silverstream, Upper Hutt. In 1953 he crossed the Tasman Sea to enter the Society of Jesus (Jesuits) at Loyola College, Watsonia, Victoria. After studying philosophy, he began his path in biblical studies by taking a combined Greek and Hebrew major in his honours degree at the University of Melbourne. Tony's artistic appreciation and keen eye for detail attracted him also to archaeology. Under the inspiration of William Culican, biblical archaeology became for a time a major interest and potential area of specialisation.

After a year's teaching at St Aloysius' (secondary) College, Milsons Point, Sydney, Tony left for Fourvière, near Lyon, France, to pursue the theological studies required for priesthood. The choice of this theological institute stemmed from the leading role played by French theologians in the rediscovery of the Bible in Catholic theology. Living and studying at Fourvière in the years immediately after the Second Vatican Council, when the shadows and memories of wartime occupation still lingered, Tony experienced the turmoil as well as the liberation that swept through such institutions at the time. The experience contributed to an abiding conviction that any theology claim-

---

1. Based on 'Antony F Campbell, SJ: A Tribute', in *Seeing Signals, Reading Signs. The Art of Exegesis. Studies in Honour of Antony F. Campbell SJ for his Seventieth Birthday,* edited by Mark A O'Brien and Howard N Wallace. Journal for the Study of the Old Testament Supplement Series 415 (London: T&T Clark International, 2004), xiii–xvi. Used with permission.

ing to be genuine must submit to a rigorous checking out against the human experience it purports to address.

Following ordination to the priesthood in July 1967, Tony moved to Rome to obtain the Licentiate in Sacred Scripture from the Pontifical Biblical Institute. The competence in biblical languages gained already in Melbourne enabled him to complete this degree in record time and then proceed to doctoral studies in Claremont, California, under the direction of Rolf Knierim. Here a fascination with biblical narrative—its genesis, its evolution, its ability to communicate meaning—was nurtured and honed into strict scholarly method, to become a life-long avocation.

One had only to meet Tony to grasp how significant a part those years in the California of the mid-1970s played in his personal, as well as his scholarly, formation. Throughout that period, he lived in the university parish of St Mary of the Angels, Claremont, where Monsignor Bill Barry was pastor for many years. A richly cultivated man, of keen theological as well as pastoral gifts, Barry offered both academic and physical hospitality to a whole generation of priest graduate students at Claremont. Tony's debt to him and to the parish community is shown by his return, time and time again, when on study leave, to that same community, and to the friendship and companionship it offered.

His Claremont doctorate gained (and soon to be published in the SBL Monograph series as The Ark Narrative [1975]), Tony returned to Australia in 1975 to teach Older Testament at Jesuit Theological College, Parkville, (JTC) within the United Faculty of Theology and the wider ambit of the Melbourne College of Divinity. Because of his theological studies in France, Tony had not been part of the foundation generation of students at JTC. He adapted, nonetheless, with alacrity to its distinctive style of living, finding that it offered an appropriate balance between community participation and the freedom required for continued scholarly work at the highest level.

Immediately on joining the faculty, Tony became Dean of JTC, a position he held for many years. Here he made a truly lasting administrative contribution. Prior to his arrival the organisation of studies reflected the upheaval in theology unleashed by Vatican II—rather much a time when 'each one did what was good in their own eyes' (Jdg 21:25). JTC had also just become a full member of the United Faculty of Theology and much work needed to be done to bring its course requirements into line with those of the other colleges and, in particular, the Bachelor of Theology degree of the Melbourne College of Divinity. With his clarity of vision, capacity for organisation, and concern to see prescription include due allowance for individual need and exception, Tony devised a pattern of structures that endured, with remarkably little revision. Successors in administration, over thirty years, merely tinkered with the arrangements he set in place.

Besides administration, first as Dean and later as Principal of Jesuit Theological College (at times holding both offices simultaneously), Tony's main contribution was as teacher of Older Testament. From the start, students in his classes, in both introductory courses and those of higher level, found themselves in the hands of a gifted and exciting teacher, effectively relating texts from a faraway past to universal human concerns and preoccupations. A scholar of international standing was mediating to them through his own formation under Knierim a tradition going back to the great German scholars of the 19th century. For many years, along with his former graduate student and long-time associate, Mark O'Brien, OP, Tony ran a research seminar on biblical narrative. This seminar forged a whole generation of students, including some of no great achievement hitherto, into a collective research team. The results of this cooperation emerged in a series of scholarly publications, notably the monumental study of source criticism, *Sources of the Pentateuch* (Fortress: 1993) and its later companion, Unfolding the Deuteronomic History (Fortress: 2000), both with Mark as co-author. Tony's research seminar has a lasting place in UFT history—and legend!

At a higher level still, Tony had a steady stream of doctoral candidates enter into the scholarly guild under his direction. Attending an overseas conference some years back, he was bemused and not entirely ungratified to hear talk of a 'Campbell-Schule'. His gifts for analysis and sense of process guided many students through research thickets to academic pastures that truly matched their capacities. The same gifts, along with a high concern for fairness and due process, made him a valued and challenging contributor on boards and in meetings associated with the Melbourne College of Divinity and other academic meetings. In recognition both of his scholarly attainment and the esteem in which he is held by his peers, the College in 1994 conferred upon him its highest award, the Doctorate of Divinity.

Tony was most generous in placing his flair for organisation and the preparation of material for publication at the disposal of various scholarly associations. He was for many years secretary of the Fellowship for Biblical Studies (Melbourne), whose academic journal, the Australian Biblical Review, he set up in print-ready copy for over two decades. He was an active member and office bearer in the Australian Catholic Biblical Association. Along with his publications, his participation in these and similar bodies contributed to ensuring that Australian biblical scholarship operated at the highest international standards.

Tony always sought, both in writing and in external lectures, workshops and the like, to make his scholarship available to a wider audience. An interest in psychology led him to work for many years on an interdisciplinary basis with Professor Edmond Chiu of Melbourne University Department of Psychiatry. He also brought biblical insights to the area of grief counselling, particularly in association with Sr Nicole Rotaru, RSM. His publication, *God First Loved Us: The Challenge of Unconditional Love* (Paulist: 2000), drew on a keen perception of human experience to communicate in engaging and accessible terms something in which he passionately believes: God's unconditional love. Many have found the book transforming.

Behind all this lay something that anyone who knew Tony well would readily concede. While he could at times present a formidable front—particularly if stirred early in the day—Tony was possessed of a deeply compassionate heart. Many are those who approached him— often in the dead of night or wee hours of morning—with some deep burden and came away feeling welcomed, heard, understood, wisely counselled. Tony's capacity for process was never more effectively in play than in such situations. In a non-judgemental and non-directive way, he sat down and helped trapped and troubled people find possibilities, ways to go, and the appropriate order in which to take them. Women, particularly those bruised and hurt in the name of religion, found in him not only great reserves of compassion but also high capacity for friendship and support. It was here that Tony's scholarship, priesthood and human qualities flowed together in a rich unity.

Besides his work as scholar and teacher, Tony for some years had oversight over the financial affairs of the Australian Jesuit province, of which he was for over fifty years a well-loved and respected member. His vigorous and colourful personality was widely held to belie the adage that all the 'characters' in the community have long since died out. While long committed to teaching and working on an ecumenical basis, his loyalty to the Catholic tradition and to the Society of Jesus within that tradition was patent. It is my privilege to pay tribute to Tony as colleague, teacher and pastor—and altogether memorable human being.

InterfaceTheology 7/1 2021

Funeral Homily

Mark O'Brien, OP

It is a great honour to preach at Tony's funeral mass and I would like to thank Fr Brian McCoy, SJ for inviting me. Our three Scripture readings—of which the passage from Romans and from John's Gospel were chosen by Tony himself, while the passage from Isaiah was chosen by myself, Nicole Rotaru and Chris Willcock—provide a rich context for us to reflect on and celebrate the life of our friend and brother, in particular his life as a member of the Society of Jesus. His calling to be a Jesuit involved moving from his home country of New Zealand to Australia, and to our proud but currently sad city of Melbourne. I can imagine that, in wrestling with his response to God's call, Tony may well have said something like Nathanael in John's Gospel—Can any good come out of Melbourne? Like Nathanael he was a man without deceit and remained a man without deceit throughout out his life, as many of us can testify. Tony always strove to present as accurate an understanding of something or someone as he could, including himself. But whatever Tony may have honestly thought and said about Australia and Melbourne, God saw him under the NZ equivalent of a fig tree and called him. Despite questions and reservations about this 'God forsaken country' (the opinion of a nineteenth century English visitor), he came and, like the biblical Nathanael, became a loyal disciple of Jesus and of Ignatius of Loyola for the rest of his life.

The first reading from Isaiah offers us a point of entry for reflecting on what was probably a key aspect of Tony's vocation as a Jesuit priest, and a key focus of his mission to the church and the world. I'm sure Tony would have gladly echoed the declaration of the servant in the passage from Isaiah, 'The Lord has given me the tongue of a teacher, that I may know how to sustain the weary with a word'. And not only the weary but also the wretched. As a loyal disciple of Jesus and Ignatius, Tony was able to bring much good out of miserable Melbourne in both word and deed. His words took two forms; the oral form in those stimulating lectures and seminars that he gave at Jesuit Theological College and the United Faculty of Theology, as well as at other places, and the written form in his many publications that achieved not only local but international recognition and acclaim. His deeds or achievements may be identified in the many students that he helped to educate, both within and outside his order, and who, with his help, acquired the knowledge and confidence to further the work of Christian discipleship. He did not teach them to be images of himself or only reflect his thinking; he taught them to be disciples of Christ, no matter what the cost.

The understanding of Christian discipleship that he fostered by his teaching and the example of his own life was above all marked by that pervasive honesty that won Jesus' praise of Nathanael. May I offer an example from my own period of being taught by Tony. When he was supervising my doctoral thesis, I assembled what I thought was an acceptable penultimate draft and sent it to him for review. His response arrived a short time later; it was brief but hit the nail right on the head. 'That's a good description of what scholars are saying O'Brien, but where's your thesis'? Now while this made me feel rather weary of the task ahead, it also sustained me in that I knew—when he was satisfied that I had a thesis to present, it would pass the toughest examination because it had already passed his scrutiny.

This leads me to make another point about Tony Campbell, and one that draws on our second reading from Paul's letter to the Romans. This is his commitment to his order, his brother Jesuits, the church, his students, and indeed society at large. I believe it was because Tony sincerely believed Paul's declaration, 'neither death, nor life, nor angels nor rulers, nor things present, nor things to come, nor powers, nor heights, nor depths, nor anything else in all creation, will be able to separate us from the love of God in Christ Jesus our Lord' that he was able to devote himself completely to his vocation as a Jesuit and Teacher of Scripture. I know from my own experience that he was completely committed to me as a student and that an important factor in this commitment was his fond hope that, once I was trained, we would become co-workers in the teaching vocation, collaborators in research and writing. That is, I myself could become a teacher in the service of those who are taught. I am sure many other students of his would confirm this. This commitment did not mean that Tony was unfailingly nice and flattering to me or other students; he was too honest for that. Rather, his commitment meant that he felt obliged to tell you how he honestly thought you were doing, or not doing. In doing so he was of course imitating in his own human way the portrayal of the God of the Older Testament, whose unswerving commitment to Israel was often expressed in the form of blunt confrontation about its sins. But no matter how bad the sins, and according to some texts they were at times very bad, and no matter how severe the punishment decreed for such sins, God never gives up on God's commitment to Israel and its mission to mediate blessing to the world. In our terms, we would say that God hates sin but loves the sinner unconditionally. And, may I say, this includes the devil. Jesus never destroys a demon in the Gospels; instead he orders them to clear off so that the possessed person may be free.

I hope I am right in this next point, but my preceding one about God's commitment to a flawed people touches on a key factor in Tony's theology and it is captured succinctly by that famous statement in our responsorial psalm; 'When I look at the heavens the work of your fingers, the moon and the stars that you established; what are human beings that you are mindful of them, mortals that you care for them? Yet you have made them little less than God, and crowned them with glory and honour'. He continually wrestled with the great question posed by the psalmist here. How can this often unreliable, even evil creature that lives a few years and then dies and rots in the earth be described as godlike or divine, and so be a, or the, key sign of the presence of God in our world? I think Tony knew that he would probably never come up with a satisfactory answer in this life but he never gave up the quest. Even when mortally ill in Nazareth House and his voice fading to a whisper, he would still, when able to, engage this great debate. It was an expression of his commitment to the faith and a further example of this man as a disciple in whom there was no deceit. In a way he was like Job, pursuing God for an answer to pressing questions that in a way became more urgent the more pain and suffering he had to endure. But his questioning was always done in a way that acknowledged God as God, the completely other, the ultimate mystery that is forever unfolding in our world of thought and feeling. The commitment to live one's life in loyalty to God despite such an awareness is surely one of the factors that contributes to the glory and honour with which God has crowned the human being— according to Psalm 8. Tony's attitude is also a further example of Paul's declaration in our reading from Romans. Nothing, not even the experience of 'the dark night of the soul' could ever separate Tony from God. He could confidently and even aggressively ask all kinds of questions of God because of his conviction of 'the love of God in Christ Jesus'.

One of the key factors that helped shape the man we fondly remember and celebrate today was of course his study of the Sacred Scriptures, especially the Older Testament. As a student of the Sacred Texts he joined the Master Class of theology and was taught not only by the one whom we believe is the ultimate author of Scripture, God, but also by God's disciples who had been entrusted with the task of teaching the world about God and God's purpose, and of living out that purpose themselves to the best of their ability. I refer here to the chosen people Israel, and in particular to those Israelites who, according to the Bible, were sent to teach and instruct Israel at strategic points in its history. Chief among these are prophets such as Moses, Samuel, Elijah, as well as those who shaped and edited the stories about them. By listening carefully to the speeches attributed to the prophets and the stories about them, Tony learned how the human being who is obedient to God and God's ways also becomes the most creative of human beings. These biblical characters emerge from the biblical text as examples of the human being made in the divine image and likeness. As such they were and are creative in a powerful yet human way, and in being obedient in a creative way, God crowns them with glory and honour, despite accounts that at times they failed their vocation. They become enduring models for readers of any generation to emulate in their own lives.

Their disciple and God's disciple, our brother Tony, was inspired by reading about them to also become creative as an interpreter and teacher of the Scriptures. In my judgement, one of his most creative contributions was the proposal of what he called 'the reported story'. By paying careful attention to narrative texts he became convinced that they are not a word-for-word record but rather the outline or report of stories that served as a basis and guide for a live performance before an audience. People in biblical times did not read silently as we tend to do. In fact, many could not read and so the written text provided a base for an oral proclamation of a story, one that would have been suitably dramatic and theatrical in order to engage and challenge an audience. Hence, scribes skilfully recorded what they heard in a way that provided opportunities for a storyteller to develop in the course of oral performance, or that provided options for a storyteller to choose from, depending on the audience. Thus, there are three ways in which the garden of Eden story can be told, two ways in which the story of David and Goliath can be told. Insights like these were then transformed into a more technical form in Tony's study of the dramatic relationship between prophets and kings in his ground breaking 1986 study *Of Prophets and Kings* and in his subsequent commentary on the books of Samuel and other books.

The hypothesis of the reported story, along with other insights into the nature of the biblical text, convinced Tony that one of God's aims in providing the Scriptures is to stimulate us to be creative listeners and readers, albeit in an authentic way that respects the text, and so to become authors and teachers like the characters presented in the Bible, like our servant in the first reading from the book of Isaiah. We believe the Bible is the Word of God but it is expressed in human words and therefore limited like all human words. It invites and indeed needs to be expounded on and explained in creative yet authentic ways. In this way the biblical word lives on in the spoken and written words of disciples throughout the generations.

But while encouraging readers and listeners to become loyal authors and teachers like the biblical characters Moses and Elijah, the Bible also reminds us that we never stop being students who need to be taught. This is a key mark of the disciple who is without guile. And given that we are godlike and always growing in the image and likeness of God, then these dual roles of the teacher who needs to be taught continue for all eternity. After all there is no end to the unfolding mystery that is God. Hence, I am sure that our beloved Tony Campbell is now gladly taking part in the heavenly seminar, the perfect form of the many seminars and classes that he conducted during his earthly life. I am also sure that this Nathanael, in whom there was and still is of course no deceit, is giving as good as he gets, is teaching as well as being taught, in the most friendly and supportive environment of course.

InterfaceTheology 7/1 2021

Antony (Tony) Campbell, SJ—A Memoir

Bill Uren, SJ

Tony Campbell died on August 2nd 2020. He was a long-time a-dying. For his was one of those difficult cases where medical and nursing care, appropriate though they were, prolonged the dying rather than enhanced the living. All this Tony endured with admirable, indeed, remarkable, fortitude and courage. For a person as independent and self-reliant as Tony, to be rendered virtually immobile in bed, to be requiring assistance to eat, to wash, to toilet, even to move, was a submission of heroic proportions. Perhaps he did rage against the dying of the light—I do not know. All I do know is that whenever I visited him at Nazareth House his equanimity and acceptance of the limitations of his situation were extraordinary.

So, when death finally came, it could not be but a blessing.

I first came into contact with Tony in 1954. He had preceded me by one year as a Jesuit novice at Loyola College, Watsonia, (in the city of Melbourne, Victoria) then the Jesuit house of formation for the Australian and New Zealand Province of the Society of Jesus. Tony's vocation as a Jesuit was both anomalous and expected. Anomalous, to some degree at least, because he had received an excellent education at the hands of the Marist Fathers at St Patrick's College, Silverstream, in New Zealand. I never knew him to speak anything but highly of the Marist Fathers. Expected, on the other hand, because Tony had two Jesuit uncles, Basil and Lou Loughnan, both stalwart members of the Australian Province. Both were formidable characters, not unlike their nephew. Basil was a military chaplain in the Second World War, and Lou was remembered as a genial and respected Rector and schoolmaster.

When I entered the novitiate Tony was assigned by the Novice Master, Edward, 'Ned' Riordan, the office of 'Prefect of Outdoor Manuals'. This involved coordinating the resources of the twenty-eight first and second year novices in maintaining the grounds of Loyola College. His managerial and administrative skills were in evidence even in those early years. Ninety minutes, five days a week, we mowed lawns, chipped weeds, maintained the septic tank, dug in the college orchard, even occasionally under supervision we were permitted to operate the mechanical hoe. On the other two days of the week, Wednesdays and Sundays, we played games, soccer, then a neutral game between those from the rugby states, NSW and Queensland, and those of us from the Australian Rules states of Victoria, South and Western Australia. To say that Tony was not a skilled player would be kind. But what he lacked in skill he more than made up for in enthusiasm—at times, as later at Campion when we played basketball, a veritable cannonball, as the bruises of his opponents, and sometimes even of his team members, could attest!

Tony graduated from the novitiate in February, 1955, and was directed to studies in the humanities: English Literature, Church History, Latin, Greek, Theory of Education, all under the benign eye of Father Noel Ryan, at Loyola College. Tony delighted and excelled at these studies, and I suspect it was in this context that Father Ryan first recognized that Tony's scholarly capabilities were of no mean order.

After a year of humanities, Tony embarked on the three-year course in scholastic philosophy—again an internal course at Loyola College. Here Tony engaged with one of his first mentors, Father Pat McEvoy, a rough-hewn and frequently unkempt professor of philosophy in the renewed scholastic tradition of Joseph Maréchal, SJ, and the transcendentalists. Tony embraced McEvoy and Maréchal enthusiastically. Within the narrow confines of that declining scholastic tradition Tony was a very competent philosopher, certainly among the best of the late fifties cohort.

So, it was something of a surprise when in 1959, instead of transitioning to further studies at the University of Melbourne, Tony was appointed to the teaching staff of Saint Aloysius College in Sydney. It was a diverse Jesuit community of ten priests and four scholastics ministering with their lay colleagues to over 1000 boys in primary, middle and secondary school. There were a number of quite eccentric characters, even by Jesuit standards, among the community, and when Tony came to Campion College the following year, he would regale us with stories of their eccentricity. One I particularly remember is of the aged Jesuit who used to wash his false teeth in his breakfast cup of tea - time-saving, indeed - but somewhat challenging to other assembled members of the community and of doubtful efficacy.

When Tony did come in 1960 to Campion Hall, the community for Jesuits studying at the various Melbourne universities, he was a marked man. The Dean of Studies was Father Noel Ryan, SJ, the same Dean who had supervised his studies in the humanities at Loyola College five years previously. Noel was a visionary, and he was aware of Tony's intellectual capabilities. His vision extended to the prospective needs of the Australian Province over the next fifty years. So, Brendan Byrne was assigned to studies that would equip him to become a New Testament scholar of international renown, Andrew Hamilton studied Russian and Greek to prepare him for ecumenical relations with Greek and Russian Orthodoxy, and Tony was directed to studies that would prepare him to succeed Father John Scullion, SJ, in lecturing and writing on the Older Testament.

It was not an easy assignment. Tony did have a rudimentary knowledge of Greek, but Hebrew, Semitic studies generally and Biblical Archaeology were altogether virgin fields for him. Studying two virtually new languages simultaneously was certainly no sinecure. Only a student of Tony's remarkable tenacity could have achieved the honours and distinctions that marked his progress through his undergraduate degree. The Professor of Middle Eastern Studies, John Bowman, was a demanding and somewhat eccentric taskmaster of Scots descent who allowed Tony little latitude. More helpful and understanding was biblical archaeologist, Bill Culican, whose investigations and hypotheses provided a welcome alternative to the rigours of mastering a range of Semitic languages.

Tony emerged with a first-class honours degree, and no doubt was anticipating a more relaxed scholarly regime in completing his theological studies at Canisius College in Sydney. Noel Ryan, however, stepped in again. The French theologians had been at the forefront of the reforms at the Second Vatican Council, especially in the area of biblical research and theology. The Jesuit theologate at Fourvière in Lyons was abreast with these developments, so where better for an ·erging Older Testament scholar to complete his theological for- ·n than in such a fertile context? So, in late 1964 Tony was des- ·to the south of France.

I have known Tony for over sixty years, but rarely did I hear him speak of his time in Fourvière.

Tony had delighted in the companionship of his peers at Loyola College and Campion Hall, so I cannot but think that it was more than a little challenging to be thrust into the more rarefied atmosphere of the sophisticated French theologate. He did make some friends, particularly among the other international students and he did drink deeply of the theological riches on offer, but it was there, I believe, that the steel first entered his heart. He learned, perforce, the virtues of survival and endurance. They were to stand him in good stead in the years of scholarship ahead, but it was in this less congenial context that he first learned how single-minded and solitary commitment to higher research must be. He put on his armour.

Tony was ordained in France in July, 1967, and, on completing his theological studies, he moved to Rome and enrolled at the Pontifical Biblical Institute for a two-year degree in biblical studies. Here he was joined by his great friend, Paddy Meagher, in 1969. Paddy had entered the Jesuit novitiate on the same day as Tony, and together they had progressed through the noviceship, humanities and philosophical studies at Loyola College. At the end of 1958, however, Paddy was assigned to the Australian Jesuit Mission in Hazaribagh, India. Paddy had a great gift for friendship, and there were many regrets when he left for India, seemingly, in those days, for life.

So, after the challenges of Fourvière, Tony was delighted to renew his friendship with Paddy in Rome. Paddy directed his studies to the New Testament, Tony, of course, to the Older Testament. Paddy returned from Rome to India in 1972 to take up an appointment lecturing in Biblical Studies at the Indian Jesuit theologate in Delhi. He was to return to Australia on many occasions, however, particularly to Perth, where he gave seminars in the Catholic Pastoral Institute for a number of years virtually on an annual basis.

From Rome Tony moved in 1971 to Claremont, California, there to undertake doctoral studies under the demanding direction of Professor Rolf Knierim, a disciple of Gerhard von Rad, one of the foremost exponents of the Form Criticism school of biblical interpretation. Knierim, too, applied this method, in particular to the historical books of the Older Testament. Tony's was one of over thirty doctoral dissertations that Knierim supervised at the Claremont Graduate School of Theology between 1965 and 1997.

This time at Claremont, I believe, was a very important period in Tony's life. After half a lifetime jumping through other people's academic hoops, now with a supervisor of his own choosing in an area of research in which these were opportunities to make significant advances, Tony was able to consolidate on the foundations he had already laid for a life in scholarship and research. It was a period of intense and vigorous research under a demanding supervisor, but one that set the standard for all Tony's subsequent contributions to biblical scholarship. He was not to be satisfied with half measures.

During this time, Tony lived in the university parish of St Mary of the Angels, supported by the hospitality of Monsignor Bill Barry and the local parish community. In return, Tony was able to exercise a priestly ministry in the parish. He discovered that he had a gift for pastoral guidance and spiritual direction. Although there was a formidable exterior—he was not an easy mark—genuine cases found in Tony wise, understanding and compassionate support.

It was here, too, that he first met Felician Sister, Feliz Gil-Jimenez, and formed with her the deepest friendship of his life. She was, at least partially, the reason why he kept returning virtually exclusively to Claremont for his sabbaticals. For forty-seven years they communicated on a daily basis, usually at length. Feliz certainly pierced the armour that Tony's unwavering commitment to scholarship and research had built up over the long years of studies and isolation. What was to become a central theme in his non-biblical writings, the unconditional love—of God, of friends—was first learned at Feliz' hands. She emancipated him from the bubble of austere scholarly relationships.

Tony returned to Australia in 1975 to Jesuit Theological College in Parkville, inner-suburban Melbourne. Jesuit Theological College was a calculated gamble on the part of the Australian Jesuit Province. It represented a commitment to ecumenical, rather than sectarian, theology, engaging with Anglican and Uniting Church colleagues in the United Faculty of Theology, (UFT), one of several colleges of the Melbourne College of Divinity. When Tony arrived, the formalities of integrating the Jesuit College into UFT had only recently been concluded, and there was much work to be done in aligning the Jesuit studies programme with the ecumenical protocols of the UFT. While there was lots of goodwill, the detail also needed to be addressed.

Enter Tony, Professor of the Older Testament and Dean of the Jesuit Faculty. Cometh the hour, cometh the man! Tony obviously had extensive experience of the ways in which faculties of theology operated, but he brought to his appointment as dean not only that but also his own personal, administrative and managerial skills. It is tempting to say that he operated administratively as rigorously as he pursued his scholarly research. He was not satisfied with half measures, and even his ecumenical colleagues at the UFT, skilled in the cut and thrust of synodal procedures, came to respect both his practice and his insights.

In the middle of 1990s the Roman authorities, perhaps alerted by the 'temple police'—right wing Catholics sniffing out potential deviations from Roman prescriptions—instituted an inquiry into the Catholicity of the theology being communicated in the ecumenical context of the United Faculty. Tony's response on behalf of the Jesuit faculty was a dissertation on the nature of the theological scholarship. It was detailed and systematic, it drew on comparisons with theologates of unimpeachable orthodoxy, it even subtly insinuated that the presuppositions on which the Roman inquiry was based were at least blinkered, if not anti-intellectual. The Roman authorities sent a lame letter in response, and no censures were entered against the Jesuit involvement.

Tony took his administrative responsibilities very seriously. He was certainly very formidable, even confrontational, in committee, both with his Jesuit and ecumenical colleagues. Academic committees in the tertiary sector are notorious for their argumentative character, and Tony was no stranger to their cut and thrust. He was sedulous both in preparing for the agenda and marshalling his arguments, and he was not easily persuaded otherwise. If you disagreed with him, you might even say he was stubborn!

All this time, of course, Tony was relentless in pursuing scholarship and research. Each time a new book emerged he would send me a copy, and I attended so many book launches where his colleagues attested to the thoroughness of his research and the perspicacity of his insights. Even though biblical scholarship was to me unknown country, just to dip into Tony's books was to become engaged in systematic detective work. The text might be the word of God, but it was also the word of man, and therefore susceptible to contextualisation and investigation, 'Go, think' was Tony's mantra, and he was certainly no slouch in responding to his own imperative.

For the ten years I was in Perth our contacts were limited to annual holidays at the Jesuit holiday home at Anglesea. Each day Tony would monopolise the community phone in the afternoon for upwards of an hour to speak to Feliz, and then he would adjourn to a bluff overlooking the beach for another hour's prayer and meditation. He was not to be disturbed!

But when I came back to Melbourne in 1987, we would meet more than occasionally for drinks in my flat at Newman and then dinner in Lygon Street. Michael Stoney and Peter Steele made up the initial quartet before Michael moved to Sydney and later, of course, Peter died prematurely. Michael Kelly, too, was a not infrequent visitor when he was is Melbourne, and Peter, and then Tony, were his spiritual directors. Michael and Tony were always sparring partners, the interchanges were often very direct, and sometimes the language was not only loud and opinionated but also sprinkled with epithets one would not have expected of priestly conviviality. Indeed, in later years when I was entrusted with making the booking, I had to take care to remember which restaurants we had recently patronised and ensure that we went to a different restaurant each time. Otherwise, I suspect, we might have incurred the embarrassment of being refused entrance. I always asked for a table at the back, isolated from the other patrons!

I was completely unaware of Tony's medical history, so it came as a shock when I heard he had been admitted to hospital for something that seemed like a stroke. I remember visiting him at the Royal Melbourne rehabilitation centre at Royal Park and then at St George's in Cotham Road, Kew, before he finally became a resident at Nazareth House. When he was on the lower floor he continued with his research as much as he was able, but even this became impossible as his condition deteriorated, and he was moved into more intensive care. Unfortunately, the Melbourne lockdown situation made it increasingly difficult to visit at Nazareth House, but I must pay tribute to the fidelity of Michael Head and Nicole Rotaru who were unremitting in exploiting whatever leeway was permitted.

My last visit was a few days before he died. Tony was still alert, but words were monosyllabic and difficult. All one could do was reminisce, and then Tony's occasional smile and murmur sufficed. The end was near, and Tony embraced it without regret, not 'raging' but 'gentle' he went 'into that good night'. The unconditional love of God was the steadfast and unwavering belief that sustained Tony both in life and in death.

Bill Uren, S.J.
Newman College
University of Melbourne

InterfaceTheology 7/1 2021

An Unusual Collection of Shaping Experiences

Michael Kelly, SJ

Father Antony ('Tony') Francis Campbell SJ, died 2 August 2020 in Victoria, Australia, aged 85 years. He joined the Jesuits in 1953. Tony wrote fourteen books on his own and three in collaboration with his close friend, the Dominican Old Testament scholar, Mark O'Brien. He established himself as a world specialist in the 'historical books', especially Samuel and Kings. He also wrote a great deal on the Pentateuch, on Job and on literary aspects of Old Testament scholarship.

A Valediction Provoking Meditation

Tony Campbell, a First Testament scholar of international renown, was a most unusual collection of shaping experiences and native drives that might appear to contradict each other.

Always and forever a proud New Zealander, he was also an inveterate internationalist who defiantly maintained his native accent unmodified by the many other linguistic contexts he experienced and lived in, most especially France and the United States.

Tony was a 'Black letter' scholar whose world ranking exegetical mastery was put at the service of his abundant capacity to teach individuals of even modest accomplishment. He specialized in unpacking narratives while at the same time creating a rich narrative as he did so.

He was a stringent scholar who was completely fluent in ancient and contemporary languages yet able to meet searching and uncertain students exactly where they were in their underdeveloped capacities as scriptural analysts and interpreters. He was courteous gentleman who could also be as crass in his crudities as a navvy telling you just what he thought about things.

Perhaps his most disarming characteristic was his gentleness which shaped the sort of pastoral care he could offer. Tony was highly intelligent, read widely beyond his professional field and he was so articulate he could be intimidating to fragile souls. Fear of his many and sometimes awesome gifts could be a barrier to appreciating just what a gentle soul he really was.

He wasn't intimidating, of course, as anyone who engaged with him would discover. This was more apparent to women than men for whom he might represent a competitive rival and so elicit blockages to understanding him that women didn't have. They knew he was listening and, for example, his patient listening was available even as the traumatized saw no end to their painful story. His patient listening was especially available to those psychologically damaged by their experience.

What was he doing? He was doing just what he did in teaching scripture, the complementary part of his pastoral care: unpacking the narrative in the sure hope that understanding its content and contours would bring the insight that would provide lasting enlightenment.

On the surface, Tony's upbringing in the sleepy if architecturally handsome city of Christchurch would seem a poor preparation for this focus in his life. Born into a comfortably secure family, Tony looked to be well protected from life's setbacks and traumas. Wrong!

His older brother survived action against the Japanese in WW2 behind enemy lines in Burma (today Myanmar) that earnt him a New Zealand Government scholarship to Cambridge University in the UK only then to lose his life in a plane accident in New Zealand just as he was about to begin a career as a stock broker. His mentally disabled brother had to be cared for all his life before his death at a relatively young age.

And Tony was mischievously self-mocking about himself, claiming that two lines of congenital insanity met in him. To support his case, he invoked the memory of two uncles in the Jesuits one of whom was widely acknowledged in the Jesuits to be crazy.

But jokes aside, the matter of sanity and psychological balance were constant focuses of attention for Tony. He read widely in current affairs and was always up to date. But his literacy in psychotherapy was the result of more than a hobby. This focus led to his partnerships in teaching with psychiatrists with whom he exchanged insights from his own work on narrative in scriptural passages because he believed, with Sigmund Freud, that a coherent personal narrative was a key to mental health.

Freud's approach to psychoanalysis gave birth to multiple schools of psychotherapy which all more or less focused on the development of the patient's personal narrative as the way heal psychic damage. Developing a narrative dealing with experience, connecting the dots and providing a way for the patient to integrate experience and move on in their lives was what Tony sought.

Tony was nothing if not searching and intellectually honest. He was thorough, even exhausting, in his determination to pursue every question of substance right through to a conclusion that met his exacting standards. But the outcome also had to pass the 'pub' test—it had to make sense even to those not necessarily professionally quali-fied to judge.

One question he kept asking all his life was whether the assertion of a belief in God was plausible and convincing. His books on spiri-tual topics attest to that. And having given his life to the exploration of myth and the way in which a people (the People of God!) con-structed the meaningfulness of their journey, Tony knew well how much the Word of God was that 'in the words of men and women', as he would say.

So, he was well and truly alive to how narratives that were self-serving and self-aggrandizing could develop with divine authority invoked to bolster their claims and in the course of it distract from the truth. But something prevented the descent into cynicism about all and any claims resorting to the divinity to justify them.

I was privileged to be with Tony about the time I think that he first explored and then wrote to describe just why his faith carried him beyond his analytic misgivings and into the mystery of the God he believed in and gave him life. We made a retreat together at a seaside house in 1977 or 1978. The exclusive focus of the eight days' silence was on God's love for us humans.

Tony derived this priority from one of the central recommenda-tions of the Spiritual Exercises of St Ignatius Loyola: that all growth in the spiritual life is a result of God's initiative, the God who loves us before we even stir to any recognition of God's presence.

'God First loved Us' is not only the title of Tony's book coming from this period but the centerpiece of his spirituality. I was mesmerized by the focus and will forever remember the night it came home to me with the experience of a grace that still animates my own spiritual life.

It was a clear spring night and I walked out onto the balcony of where we were staying. The sea was rolling and breaking nearby and I looked up into the sky to behold the infinite expanse of a sky teeming with stars and the light of a fading moon.

I kept staring and realised for the first time—I must have been twenty-five—that I had never held my stare at the sky that long because at some subterranean level I feared the sky would come tumbling in on me.

I didn't and as never before I felt I had made peace with the universe. Why? Because it was the work of God who first loved us.

I shared the experience with Tony and knew for the first time just what his own mysticism did to enrich and sustain his own embrace of the mystery of God, a mystery he sought to be with till his last breath on earth

Innovative Perspectives on the Pentateuch

Sarah L Hart

This essay addresses Antony Campbell's contribution to Pentateuchal research on the international arena. As I was Tony's final doctoral student and worked on a section of text in the middle of the Pentateuch, Exodus 24:15—Numbers 10:28 I was approached to write on Tony's ideas apropos the Pentateuch.[1] One of the skills that Tony expected of a student was to render succinctly and fairly the ideas of a scholar. With this standard in mind I present in my own words what I understand to be some of Tony's most challenging ideas on the Pentateuch. I start by looking briefly at Tony's biblical training then I move chronologically through his publications focusing on those that deal with the Pentateuch. In the postlude I share some experiences of Tony as a supervisor. Throughout the essay the liberty is taken of writing of Antony F Campbell as Tony.

Biblical Training

Tony knew the background of most scholars whose works he had read so it is appropriate in turn to briefly address Tony's biblical background—a training in biblical languages, archaeology, and form-criticism. Tony did his doctoral studies at the University of Claremont, California, with Rolf Knierim (1928–2018) (1928-2018), a student of Gerhard a student of Gerhard von Rad (1901–1971), University of Heidelberg, Germany. Tony was proud of this biblical lineage in form-criticism which goes back to von Rad. Form-criticism is an exegeti-

---

1. Published as Sarah L Hart, *From Temple to Tent: From Real to Virtual World (Exodus 24:15—Numbers 10:28)* (Adelaide: ATF Theology, 2019).

cal method that examines typical forms and genres, their settings and functions. Tony's most classic applications of form-criticism are his *1 Samuel* and *2 Samuel* commentaries published in the Forms of Old Testament Literature series, a commentary series dedicated to publishing form critical method applied to each book of the Old Testament[2]

Focus of Form Criticism on the Final Text and Oral Tradition

Form criticism deals with the final text, that is, the text before the reader. It also addresses material in the final text which shows signs of oral traditions and thereby suggests earlier traditions. Attempts at reconstructing oral traditions and their settings are made by peeling away the alleged layers of editorial comment, editorial composition, and undoing the organisation of the textual material in the final text. The titles of Tony's later books reflect his interest in addressing original or early traditions in the biblical writings from a fresh stance. *Rethinking the Pentateuch* concerns thinking about the stories of the Pentateuch evolving from different oral traditions, not stories within a blending of four different sources.[3] *Genesis Beyond Sources* is a more recent publication with a similar focus, again trying to leave behind the shackles of the four-source theory or more recent variants thereof.[4] In these books Tony offers a new way of viewing the ancient Hebrew stories of the Pentateuch.

A Major Paradigm for Reading the Pentateuch until 2005

Source Theory

Until the late 1700s plain or literal reading was the standard way to read biblical texts. For example, persons mentioned in the biblical text were more or less understood as historical people. Lineage and names in genealogies were generally accepted. God spoke in some

---

2. Antony F Campbell, *1 Samuel*, FOTL Vol VII (Grand Rapids, Mich: Eerdmans, 2003), and *2 Samuel*, FOTL Vol VIII (Grand Rapids, Mich: Eerdmans, 2005).

3. Antony F Campbell and Mark A O'Brien, *Rethinking the Pentateuch: Prolegomena to the Theology of Ancient Israel* (Louisville, Ky: Westminster John Knox Press, 2005).

4. Antony F Campbell, *Genesis Beyond Sources: A New Approach* (Adelaide: ATF Theology, 2018).

instances directly to people. What was related was understood as an event that had occurred in real time. If ambiguities in the texts were observed they tended to be harmonised and sense made of the whole. The 1800s mark the start of so-called modern biblical scholarship. Some European scholars with knowledge of Semitic languages observed variations within the biblical texts, noting different names for God and listing redundancies or repetitions of the texts within the books of, in particular, the Pentateuch. The differences and duplications were analysed as stemming from different sources. Out of this research came the theory that the Pentateuch is made up of four different sources. With time the four-source theory gained precedence over reading the Pentateuch as made up of five books.

One of the most accepted analyses of the four-source theory is that of Martin Noth. Tony, in collaboration with Mark O'Brien, a former doctoral student turned friend, had the idea that each source, according to Noth's analyses, be printed in full. This insight led to each source being printed as an unbroken document instead of the usual lists of references to biblical book, chapter, and verse. Readers could then clearly observe the beginning of each source and follow the sequence of the contents until the end. The result is *Sources of the Pentateuch* (1993) wherein three of four sources as identified by Martin Noth—the Priestly document, the Yahwist narrative, and the Elohist texts—are laid out in full in the translation of the New Revised Standard Version.[5]

Sources of the Pentateuch has become a standard reference book for courses on the Pentateuch which address diachronic methods and source theory. A general introduction facilitates an understanding of source theory and before each of the three sources printed in full are also introductory notes. In the final chapter, three composite texts that have become classic examples of the source theory are discussed and interpreted—the Flood Story (Gen 6:5–9:17), the Beginning of the Joseph Story (Gen 37:1–36) and Deliverance at the Sea (Exod 13:17–31). In my view Tony and O'Brien are neither for nor against the source theory. They had the foresight to make the material of source theory easily accessible for study of the sources. As Kurt

---

5.   Antony F Campbell and Mark A O'Brien, *Sources of the Pentateuch: Texts, Introductions, Annotations* (Minneapolis: Fortress, 1993). The fourth source, the book of Deuteronomy designated by the acronym D is not printed out in *Sources of the Pentateuch*.

Aland's *Synopsis of the Four Gospels* facilitates study of the gospels, so Tony and O'Brien's *Sources of the Pentateuch* is an invaluable teaching and research resource for studies of the Pentateuch.[6]

A New Model Proposed for Reading the Pentateuch by Campbell and O'Brien

Text-as-Base-for-User

Twelve years after *Sources of the Pentateuch* (1993), Tony's next major book on the Pentateuch is a further collaboration with Mark O'Brien, a 183 page work, *Rethinking the Pentateuch: Prolegomena to the Theology of Ancient Israel* (2005).[7] The ideas in this new work depart from general scholarly acceptance of the 1878 four source theory as formulated by Wellhausen, from the sources as laid out in *Sources of the Pentateuch* according to Noth's analysis, and also from more recent variants of the theory. Tony and O'Brien propose an alternative model—that base story units are contained within the cycles on Abraham and Jacob or in narratives such as the exodus from Egypt and the construction of the sanctuary. The units require fleshing out. Each biblical story is too short to be regarded as a record of a telling or performance but the various short units extant in the final text can be treated as material for a storyteller to work with.[8] Tony and O'Brien call these short textual units that require developing, or expounding, 'text-as-base-for-user'. They were the basis for story telling by a storyteller in the oral culture of ancient Israel. The new idea launched in *Rethinking the Pentateuch* was that of 'text-as-base-for-user'. *Rethinking the Pentateuch* was reviewed by scholars such as Thomas Römer or Thomas Dozeman in the *Review of Biblical Literature* but Tony felt his ideas were misunderstood by them.[9] Thereafter, in the majority of essays and books, in particular *Genesis Beyond Sources* (2018), he presents in more detail and with further examples, the ideas outlined in *Rethinking the Pentateuch* (2005).

---

6. *Synopsis of the Four Gospels* (edited by Kurt Aland: USA: United Bible Societies, 1981).
7. (Louisville, Ky: Westminster John Knox Press).
8. *Rethinking the Pentateuch*, 16.
9. Thomas B Dozeman (4 pages) https://www.bookreviews.org/pdf/4963_5209.pdf and Thomas Römer (3 pages) https://www.bookreviews.org/pdf/4963_5208.pdf both 03/2006 in *Review of Biblical Literature*.

Tony's work on the Pentateuch in more recent years offers new perspectives on the so-called final text and readdresses the paradigm of text-as-base-for-user. These new perspectives are addressed in the next section, starting with different ways to think about the final text.

Editing Collapses Diversity into Unity[10]

Tony sees some of the editing process as the imposing of unity on diverse material. As national identity diminishes with increasing globalisation or local government loses influence when state control dominates thus bringing stories together from different sources into one compilation diminishes the original diversity. Compiling makes different stories seem as though they belong together, or, that they are more related to one another than they were in reality. The Pentateuch is a compilation of sometimes similar but more often than not different material from different places, times, and traditions—the end product of editors. The word 'editors' is used here generically, referring to those who engaged in tasks such as editing, compiling, collating, redacting, even creatively rewriting to such a degree that some sentences may be called new writing. An effect of editors on the final text is the loss of diversity and a semblance of unity. Tony proposes that the small narrative units of the Pentateuch need to be treated as stories for the telling by an intermediary. Thereby, something of the original diversity can be tapped into and a vibrant theological approach can be re-accessed.

Viewing the Pentateuch as Chronology, not History[11]

Text critical approaches to the Pentateuch in the 1800s, as already mentioned, resulted in the theory that the Pentateuch is made up of four different sources. The source theory was presented within an historical framework. The link between source theory and an emphasis on history is evident in the titles of books that have become classics

---

10. AF Campbell, 'Trap: From Diversity to Unity' in "Pentateuch Beyond Sources: A New Paradigm" in *Opening the Bible: Selected Writings of Antony Campbell, SJ* (Adelaide: ATF Theology, 2014), 99–118.

11. AF Campbell, 'Trap: From Chronology to History' 108–109 from 'Pentateuch Beyond Sources', in *Opening the Bible*.

in the field, for example, Julius Wellhausen's *Prolegomena to the History of Israel,* or Martin Noth's *A History of Pentateuchal Traditions.*[12]

Tony moves away from the Pentateuch as made up of four sources or four mini histories, acknowledging that where the sources begin and end is often disputed. He focuses instead on different traditions, such as those of Abraham, the Abraham and Lot collection, or Rebekah to mention just three of many. Editors of the Pentateuch needed to organise the diverse material of the different cycles and traditions at their hands. They organised the material according to a chronology with a focus on parents and offspring rather than, for example, on a chronology of relations between nations or geographical locations. The point is that the Pentateuchal material of the final text was assigned a chronology but not organised as history as is suggested with the use of the word history in the titles of the works of Wellhausen and Noth mentioned in the previous paragraph. Reading the stories of the Pentateuch as history is to fall into the trap of a false chronology.

Retelling the ancient stories today, unfettered by historical sequence as Tony suggests, permits tellers and listeners to immerse themselves in the present with the development of, for example, a character trait. Tony proposes motifs or recurring thematic elements as a way of reading and interpreting between and among the stories of the Pentateuch. Possible motifs and themes for development by a storyteller from a base story are given in the many examples in *Genesis Beyond Sources.*

The Priority of the Present over the Past[13]

The printed text of a Bible today can be designated as the 'final text'. Over the centuries the words that make up the biblical texts in their final form have become fixed or orthodox. In some traditions they

---

12. Julius Wellhausen, *Prolegomena to the History of Ancient Israel,* translated by J Sutherland Black and Allan Menzies, with preface by W Robertson Smith (Edinburgh: Adam & Charles Black, 1885); translation of *Prolegomena zur Geschichte Israels,* second edition (Berlin: G Reimer, 1883). Martin Noth, *A History of Pentateuchal Traditions* (Chico, Calif: Scholars Press, 1981), translation of *Überlieferungsgeschichte des Pentateuch* (Stuttgart: Kohlhammer Verlag, 1948).
13. AF Campbell, 'Rethinking Revelation: The Priority of the Present over the Past', in *Opening the Bible,* 353–363.

are revered and elevated with ritual and theological designations such as 'The Word of God'. However, it is worth considering concepts of time when thinking of the final text. Over two thousand years ago authors or editors of the biblical texts prepared texts in the present of the period in which they lived, generally using material from the oral traditions of their past. For example, if it is accepted that most of the Pentateuch was compiled in post-exilic Babylonia or Yehud (Judea), the ancestral traditions and customary laws of the past were ordered and redacted by editors in the present of their day. The experience of the present of the authors in the post-exilic period determined how they presented, organised, and interpreted their given material and what they added to the given material (or did not use).

When the final text is read today a double form of present interpretation is at play. The authors of the biblical texts in the Pentateuch interpreted their past from the stance of their post-exilic present and we read the biblical past in terms of our present. What is in common is that the authors in the ancient world lived in their present time and we live in present time today. The theology of the editors of the traditions that make up the Pentateuch was influenced by their present and how the texts are revealed or disclosed to us today is influenced by our experience of our present. The point is that Tony's emphasis is on the involvement of people, in both ancient Israel and today. Then and now, the stories of the Pentateuch are read and interpreted with an interest in the present and the divine.

The Pentateuch—Driving Force or End of the Hebrew Biblical Writings?

In the essay, 'The Pentateuch: Guard's Van or Engine?' Tony queries the function of the Pentateuch in relation to the other writings of what he calls the Older Testament (OT).[14] The books of the Pentateuch are printed before other OT writings in a Bible. Though the writings of the Pentateuch are at the front, are they the driving force? In the metaphor of a train, the engine is the driving power at the front and the guard's van is the last vehicle at the rear, drawn by the front. The basis of this idea comes from a prevalent theory that the infancy narratives of Matthew and Luke are later additions to the main gospels.

---

14. *Opening the Bible*, 313–318.

Tony proposes that two sections of the Pentateuch, both set at Sinai, the Covenant Code (Exod 19–24) and the sanctuary unit (Exod 25—Num 10), are more recent additions to the older ancestral and exodus traditions. Furthermore, he notes that from the exodus out of Egypt onwards Israel is presented as all Israel, consisting of twelve tribes. Though 'all Israel' is presented as participating in the passage through the Reed Sea and journeying through the wilderness, modern scholarship thinks of 'all Israel' as a relatively recent construct. Tony sums up, 'Israel rummaged among the traditions of its beginnings to express something of the reality that it had come to be'.[15] This means the Pentateuch consists of old oral traditions plus new material from the editors being combined to portray a unified Israelite people. The ramifications of these observations are that the Pentateuch was compiled late and additions were made to serve as the engine of the whole train, that is as final text. Presenting Israel as unified permits entry of 'all Israel' into the promised land as recounted from Joshua forwards.

Text-as-Base-for-User

Tony's new paradigm for Pentateuchal studies is the idea of text-as-base-for-user. The stories of ancient Israel are seen as short narrative units which have been preserved and can be uncovered in the Pentateuch. They can be used as 'present text' in contrast to what may be thought of as the past or final text of a printed Bible. What the telling of stories in ancient Israel and today have in common is a live audience and a listening context. A story is living in that it is told anew by someone within a community. Tony thinks of the narratives of the Pentateuch as stories originating long ago in different parts of ancient Israel but relevant in our time. The base text, which may have functioned like an aide-mémoire, is often ten to fifteen verses. Stories need to leave the realm of silent reading and enter the world as new and living. A user-base text requires elements that can be developed. These can range from references to time or place to some indication of the motivation of the people involved. God is within the stories in a myriad of ways and the stories require an outcome.[16]

---

15. Opening the Bible, 317.

16. *Genesis Beyond Sources: A New Approach* (Adelaide: ATF Theology, 2018), 49. To date to my knowledge *Genesis Beyond Sources* has not been reviewed in scholarly journals. Though the body of the text is footnoted scholarly arguments are not pursued.

Base texts were likely developed and expanded through a user or intermediary such as a wise person, a storyteller, or a teacher in the context of ancient Israel. Today, this may be through a teacher, wise person, commentator, preacher or theologian.[17] Interpreters do not have unlimited imaginative freedom as expansion of a base text is controlled by the subject matter of the text and the community or audience listening to the telling. The telling of a story with expansion could take up to sixty minutes. The modern urban audience with a tendency to critical thinking, comparing, and analysing, may have lost the ability to let time stand still and to reflect on the present. Motifs within the base texts can be forever unpacked in new variants as the Greeks have done and modern writers or artists do with popular characters such as the mythological Electra. Through story telling a way to live in the present can be rediscovered.

Some base units are available in two versions though Tony prefers to call them base unit alternatives. The different versions invite variants, enhancements, and supplements to the base texts. Variants offer different shades of meaning. For example, two variants in the Tower of Babel story (Gen 11:1–9) are possible in verse 7. God, YHWH, is a singular subject in most of the Babel story yet in verse 7 God speaks of self-using the first-person plural pronoun 'us.' Alternatively, the storyteller could develop either God confusing the people's language (verse 7) or scattering the people (verse 8).[18] The singular versus plural variant with reference to God is also available in the unit, 'Visitors come to Abraham's Tent' (Gen 18:1–15).

Enhancements may illuminate aspects of meaning or expand understanding. For example, in the second creation account (Gen 2b–3:24), the four rivers (Gen 2:10–14) which bring fertility and abundance to the known world, illuminate the stream that has watered the earth (Gen 2:5) earlier in the unit.[19]

Supplements[20] bring in new material that can be used as in the story of Jacob meeting 'Rachel at the Well' (Gen 29:1–14) where twice in verse 10 reference is made to 'his (i.e., Jacob's) mother's brother'. The new material allows for the presentation of Rachel as Laban's daughter or as Rebekah's niece. A camera is looking at family rela-

17. *Genesis Beyond Sources*, xix–xxv.
18. *Genesis Beyond Sources*, 46.
19. *Genesis Beyond Sources*, 13.
20. *Genesis Beyond Sources*, 98.

tionships focused on Rachel rather than Jacob. The unit, Genesis 29:1-14, contains a type scene and is open to story-telling development. Various family issues such as similarities between the character of Jacob and Laban or Jacob's attraction to Laban's younger not older daughter could be developed.

From 'Word of God' to 'Word of God's People'

Tony moves the oral world of ancient Israel, twenty-five centuries ago or more, into the modern world. The final text or printed narratives of the Pentateuch are an inanimate medium as opposed to people who are a living medium. The stories become animate, or alive, when told and heard within a community in the moment of the present. In the distant past, intermediaries told, expanded, and interpreted stories about Israel and their God which can happen today when users interpret the base texts. Tony presents the stories of the Pentateuch as stories valid for today. The texts are not static or museum pieces. They need to be treated less as the Word of God and more as God working through the people telling and interpreting the stories, and the community receiving them. They are the words of God's people. It is not necessarily easy to study and ponder the content of the Pentateuch but Tony offers the challenge that we go and reflect together as the people of God. A phrase he often used to make us come alive was 'Go think!'[21]

Postlude

In this postlude I share some of my experiences of Tony as a doctoral supervisor. Tony knew I had lived in Vienna, Austria, for many years. At the first Melbourne supervision he gave me a very long indigestible German work to read—to test me, I guess but I was undaunted. I regularly emailed Tony my work and after about 12 months wrote a thesis proposal which did not really arouse his interest. I realised I was hitting my head against a wall as my thesis topic was not evolving. Tony told me how he came to his doctoral topic at Claremont. Rolf Knierim in a postgraduate class mentioned three areas that required

---

21. Antony Campbell, *Experiencing Scripture: Intimacy with Ancient Text and Modern Faith* (Adelaide: ATF, 2012).

research, one of which was the ark narrative in 1–2 Samuel. Tony said, 'I'll take that topic'. I started to hear that Tony thought research was required on the Sinai material and the portable sanctuary. I proceeded to undertake this research.

I went to two or three supervision sessions a year. The three-hour afternoon sessions, never in the morning, were punctuated with a cup of tea. Tony was collegial. I was invited to lunch at Jesuit College, Parkville and introduced to staff and fellow Jesuits. During my Melbourne visits I attended various events such as Tony's post-graduate seminars on Job or his lectures at what was then the United Faculty of Theology. Once I was his guest at a meeting of the Fellowship of Biblical Studies where I heard Amy-Jill Levine speak.

Tony liked to compare textual work to that of a classicist describing a Greek vase. An example of this is Tony and O'Brien describing the narrative texts of the Pentateuch as collections of reported stories—the gist of a story is recorded not a verbatim rendition of its performance or telling. In short, the narrative textual evidence consists of reported stories.

Tony was meticulous with work I emailed him—he immediately confirmed receipt, printed it out and saved it onto his hard drive. He made technical academic expectations clear at the start and was unimpressed when I misspelled his name once. I never misspelled it again. Biblical quotes had always to be stated—book, chapter, and verse, and then there was the difference in use of a hyphen (-), dash (–) and em dash (—). On first mention, terms had to be defined, a procedure whereby the writer is covered even if the reader does not agree with the definition. Writing techniques were later extended with reference to the *Chicago Manual of Style*.[22]

Timewise, I always gave Tony a week to email back responses to my work. This allowed him the space to choose the time that suited him. He always replied—addressing salient detail but more importantly responding with general comments and concepts.

Each supervision session left me with more than six months research. Tony did most of the talking in his famous style with two voices, a proposing voice versus an emotive counter voice (often with expletives). At many supervision sessions Tony shared with me what he was reading and his responses to that reading—fairly summaris-

---

22. 16th edition.

ing the ideas of a work but then tearing it often to shreds. Once he communicated how he felt misunderstood in reviews of *Rethinking the Pentateuch: Prolegomena to the Theology of Ancient Israel* (2005). I answered that I thought the work had an unfortunate title incorporating the word 'prolegomena',[23] that the contents were difficult to understand and that it was too densely presented thereby not giving justice to the ideas therein.

Tony knew where scholars had studied, who they studied with, and where they got jobs. He knew that a scholar's background influenced their thinking and that research and writing were supported or hindered by the given circumstances. Towards the end of supervision sessions Tony posed two or three major questions regarding my work, introduced by a change of voice which became pastoral. I do not remember any of the questions but I remember the change of voice—they indicated moving from Tony's ideas to my ideas.

Tony threw a wide range of books at me to read over various supervision sessions. Once it was David Carr's *Writing on the Tablet of the Human Heart*. Another time it was a gift of his facsimile edition of *Scrolls from Qumran Cave* 1. The gift was in response to a visit I had made to the University of Sydney to view a facsimile of the Qumran Isaiah scroll. Tony and I discussed Qumran—issues such as water sources, the distances between buildings, and the compound layout. We also discussed Israel travels—he explored Israel on a motor bike whereas I hiked parts of the Israel National trail.

From mid-2007 to mid-2008 formal studies were on hold as Tony was on sabbatical in California, USA, and I was working in an orchestra in Norrköping, Sweden. While in Europe I had the chance to visit the theology library at Humboldt University, Berlin, and access works of nineteenth century German biblical scholars—a century of extraordinary research in terms of literary textual criticism, archaeology, concepts relating to history and biblical languages study. I also had the luck to see the major exhibition *Babylon: Mythos und Wahrheit* at the Vorderasiatischen Museum, Berlin. During the long nights in Sweden time was available to make my own informal translations from German into English of the works of the German biblical scholars. I also went to post-graduate seminars at the University of Copenhagen attended by Niels Lemche and Thomas Thompson

---

23. A preliminary discussion, introductory essay to a work, a prologue.

(scholars identified with biblical minimalism). The ideas of Jan Assmann on collective memory were widely debated at the Copenhagen seminars. When supervision recommenced with Tony in late-2008 I had had a year with all these new experiences. Tony often used the metaphor of a washing machine—you threw ideas into it, it went around and round, then ideas came out. After Sweden I started writing the chapters of my thesis.

People ask, 'What questions did Tony pose?' I do not remember. Early on, I said to Tony, 'Teach me to think'. He replied, 'You can bl**** well teach yourself to think'. Unawares I did. Tony recommended books. He treated me respectfully. He encouraged me. In hindsight I realise Tony let me develop as a biblical researcher. He did not get in the way of growth. He left me space to develop and the freedom to fly. Tony was an 'enfant terrible' as regards use of language at times. He could be provocative in the way in which he challenged the ideas of others but he was also extraordinarily sensitive and pastoral.

Reflections on 2 Kings 8:1–6 and its Context
In Light of Antony Campbell's Theory of
'The Reported Story'

Mark O'Brien, OP

Within the study of the Hebrew Bible/Old Testament (HB/OT), the name and work of Antony F Campbell has been closely associated with Form Criticism. The primary aim of the instigators of Form Criticism in Germany, in particular Herman Gunkel and Hugo Gressmann, was to trace the history of a form of HB/OT literature such as a story or a poem back to its original *Sitz-im-Leben* or 'life setting'. They judged that the original life setting for most of these forms was oral and that they were short pieces. Ancient peoples generally could not read a written text, or did not have access to them, and so had to rely on their (limited) memories. Thus, literary forms were tailored to their audiences. Their analysis of the HB/OT sought to identify and set aside as later additions or expansions evidence that disturbed what they judged to be the original relatively brief oral units from which the present text subsequently developed. This concern to recover the original, and most likely, oral literary form from the present text of the HB/OT stimulated a kind of reversal in some subsequent scholarly research. That is, research into the origins of a text prompted research into how the present text emerged from such origins.

Campbell's 1975 doctoral dissertation on the so-called 'Ark Narrative' in 1 Samuel 4–6; 2 Samuel 6 established his credentials for taking part in this kind of research and pointed to the contributions that he would subsequently make to the Form Critical enterprise.[1] His application of key criteria employed by Form Criticism—namely,

---

1. Antony F Campbell, *The Ark Narrative (1 Sam 4–6; 2 Sam 6). A Form-Critical and Traditio-Historical Study*, SBLDS 16 (Missoula: Scholars Press, 1975).

what kind of a text is the one under investigation (its genre; German 'Gattung'); what was its likely life setting, and why was it composed (intention)—led him to conclude that the Ark Narrative was indeed composed from smaller units but in order to form a larger unified text within the setting of the emergent Davidic dynasty. Its intention or purpose was to mark the transition from an earlier epoch to the new one of the Davidic dynasty reigning in the new capital of Jerusalem. He readily acknowledged that a number of additions had been made to the Ark Narrative but identification of these enhanced the case for the unified nature of the underlying narrative.

Subsequent form critical analysis, in particular of narrative texts, led Campbell to propose, as noted in the chapter by Sarah Hart, what may well have been his most original contribution to the study of the HB/OT; namely his theory that narrative texts often contain what he termed a 'reported story'. As Gunkel, Gressmann and others had noted, individual HB/OT stories are often rather brief, that some have variant versions of an episode or 'doublets', that they have what seem to be gaps that need to be filled in (setting of a scene, information about a person or place, etc.), that the links between episodes in a story or between stories are sometimes not clear, and that the chronological or thematic sequences of stories are at times reversed. These features were generally explained as later redactional/editorial additions or as loose collections of once independent material. However, in a 1989 article for the journal *Semeia,* Campbell proposed that such features pointed to the written text being the report of one or more stories that could be developed in an oral performance. That is, the text formed what he called a 'user base' for storytellers.[2] His theory emerged from a close analysis of HB/OT narratives within their textual context as well as within their larger ANE context. The latter drew on the view noted above, namely, that because few people in the ancient world could read, written texts were proclaimed aloud and in a suitably dramatic manner for an audience. Also, because writing was an expensive and time-consuming operation, no scribe could record verbatim what a storyteller said. Certain items had to be abbreviated or left out, but they were most likely things that could be filled out

---

2. See Campbell, 'The Reported Story: Midway Between Oral Performance and Literary Art', in *Semeia,* 46 (1989): 77–83. Reprinted in *Opening the Bible: Selected Writings of Antony Campbell SJ* (ATF Theology: Adelaide, 2014), 365–75.

or filled in during an oral performance. The variants or doublets that one encounters in the written text could also be explained in relation to oral performance when one interpreted them as options that a storyteller could choose from to enhance a performance. [3] Whereas earlier critical analysis tended to regard the present text as a rather loose juxtaposition of stories without clear thematic or chronological links, Campbell's theory argued that the present text was arranged with a definite purpose in mind.[4]

As with most literature the analysis of biblical texts is a work of interpretation and, as Campbell noted in the Introduction to his commentary on I–II Samuel, 'The definitive interpretation of a text is out of reach' because no interpreter can take account, fully and accurately, of all the phenomena in a text, let alone all the circumstances surrounding its production. He asserted that one should not ask whether an interpretation is the right one but whether it 'is adequate and responsible'. A responsible interpretation is one 'that pays attention to the signals in the text that need to be interpreted.' An adequate interpretation is one 'that integrates all or most of these signals into a single interpretative horizon'.[5] Campbell subsequently tested his theory of the 'reported story' by applying it to the book of Genesis.[6] As a way of honouring his contribution to the study of HB/OT narrative, I will apply the theory to a text he himself did not analyse, namely 2 Kgs 8:1–6. It forms part of a collection or sequence of shorter and longer narratives about the prophet Elisha and his relationship with a variety of characters in 2 Kings 2–10 and has generated consider-

---

3. Campbell elaborated on his understanding of the reported story and the storyteller's role, and provided a number of examples, in 'The Storyteller's Role: Reported Story and Biblical Text', in *CBQ*, 64 (2002): 427–41; reprinted in *Opening the Bible*, 133–151.

4. A study that also argues for meaning and purpose in the way texts appear to have been 'juxtaposed' is that of Rachelle Gilmour, *Juxtaposition and The Elisha Cycle*, LHB/OTS 594 London: Bloomsbury T & T Clark, 2015). Her thesis is that 'biblical authors and editors deliberately used juxtaposition to shape the meaning of their narrative' (*cf* 3). Although she does not discuss Campbell's theory of the 'reported story', the two approaches share the conviction that there is meaning and purpose in the 'juxtaposition' of texts.

5. Campbell, *1 Samuel*, FOTL VII (Grand Rapids: Eerdmans, 2003), xvii.

6. See *Genesis Beyond Sources* (Adelaide: ATF Theology, 2016). He and I had earlier applied it in *Rethinking the Pentateuch. Prolegomena to the Theology of Ancient Israel* (Louisville: WJK, 2005).

able debate as to its nature and its relationship to the surrounding context.[7]

2 Kings 8:1–6 is about three of these characters and each features prominently in one or more of the preceding narratives. The first is the woman of Shunem whose son Elisha restored to life (*cf* 8:1-2, 6). The story of this miracle is told in 4:8–37. The second is Elisha's servant Gehazi (*cf* 8:4-5) who features in 4:8-37 as well as in the account of the healing of Naaman, the commander of the Aramean army, in 5:1–27. The third is the king of Israel who is mentioned in the preceding narratives about the woman (*cf* 4:13) and about Naaman (*cf* 5:5-8), but who plays a prominent role in the account of the hostilities between Aram and Israel in 6:1–7:20.[8] I would agree with commentators who judge these narratives are not simply reports of events but dramatic stories. According to Campbell what marks a story is that it is not 'driven by what happened, but by the plot around which the storyteller has chosen to weave the story'.[9] The way the plot of a story unfolds depends on the artistic creativity of the storyteller, although he or she must operate within the context of their particular language, culture and religion otherwise the audience will miss its meaning. Because a story normally moves from an introduction or initial setting to a complicating factor that drives the story towards a crisis or climax, followed by its resolution and end of story, each of the above texts may be classified as a distinct story. Each deals with a crisis—a dead child, a leprous foreigner, a war with Aram—that is resolved in a way that involves dramatic interaction between key characters.

While there is good evidence that each story is a distinct and whole unit, there is also evidence that points to limitations in each. One is that each story has some ambiguous or unresolved features.

---

7. Philip E Satterthwaite argues for the literary coherence of 2 Kings 2–8 (*cf* 'The Elisha Narratives and the Coherence of 2 Kings 2–8,' in *Tyndale Bulletin*, 49'1 [1998]: 1-28). In my judgement this overlooks the role of one of the 'sons of the prophets' in the story of Jehu in 2 Kgs 9–10 and, as I will point out in this paper, there is a link between this and Elisha's initial encounter with the 'sons of the prophets' (NRSV 'company of prophets') in 2 Kgs 2.

8. Even though the king is unnamed, within the context it is reasonable to identify him as Jehoram (also as Joram) of Israel (*cf* 2 Kgs 3:1–3). The rival Aramean king is named Ben-hadad in 6:24 and, according to 8:7–15, his reign coincided in part with that of Jehoram.

9. Campbell, *1 Samuel*, 5.

I cannot go into the details of each story in a limited paper such as this, but consideration of the following features in the first story may help to illustrate the point.[10] The description of the journey that the woman makes to Elisha after her son's death leavers a reader uncertain whether it is to beg him to raise her son or whether it is to justify herself and blame him.[11] Also, when she says to Elisha 'I will not leave without you' (4:30) is this because she believes he alone has the God-given power to raise her son, or because he is responsible for the disaster that has struck her household and he must return with her to ensure that neither she nor her husband is held responsible.[12] As well as these features, the ending of the story in 4:37 is rather abrupt, leaving the relationship between Elisha and the woman unresolved. Much the same can be said about the endings to the second and third stories in 5:27 and 7:20 respectively. This is the kind of textual evidence that led Campbell and others to see the written text as a 'user base' for a storyteller to flesh out in appropriate ways in an oral performance.

Although some commentators think 2 Kings 8:1–6 is a later addition to the text, or that it has been relocated from an earlier position elsewhere in the text, within the present textual sequence it serves to link the three originally independent stories, and it does this by providing further 'user bases' for storytellers.[13] Reflection on the passage within the context of 2 Kgs 4–8 points to a number of options that a storyteller could develop. An initial one is the way the woman obeys without question or hesitation Elisha's word in 8:1 about how

---

10. For a recent and detailed analysis of these stories see Roy L Heller, *The Characters of Elijah and Elisha and the Deuteronomic Evaluation of Prophecy. Miracles and Manipulation*, LHB/OTS 671 (London: Bloomsbury T & T Clark, 2018).

11. As she says in 4:28 'Did I ask my lord for a son? Did I not say, Do not mislead me'?

12. An additional contextual factor that complicates matters here is that her resolve not to leave without Elisha recalls Elisha's earlier resolve in 2:4, 6 not to leave Elijah, despite the latter's assertion that he has to journey alone.

13. On 8:1–6 as a later addition, see the review of literature in Martin Mulzer, 'Der kranke und der gesunde Gehasi. Zum Verhältnis von 2 Kön 5 zu 2Kön 8, 1–6', in *Biblische Notizen, Neue Folge*, 153 (2012): 19–27, especially 23. Among those who think the passage has been relocated we may note JA Montgomery, *The Books of Kings*, ICC (Edinburgh T & T Clark, 1951), 591; and M Cogan and H Tadmor, *II Kings*, AB 11 (Garden City, NY: Doubleday, 1988), 87. According to these commentators it originally functioned as a continuation of 4:8–37.

to escape the looming famine. This is in marked contrast to her response to his earlier promise of a son. A storyteller could expatiate on her transformation from being resistant and even rejecting to being obedient by telling how the raising of her son convinced her that Elisha was a true prophet, not a deceptive one. Moreover, the death and restoration to life of her son was a forerunner or sign that as long as she obeyed his word, she and her household would escape the death of famine and be restored to a new life in their land after seven years. Furthermore, the report of the encounter between the woman and the king in 8:6 would allow a storyteller to recount how her post-famine restoration took place. In relation to this, some commentators have argued that the exchange between Gehazi and the king in vv 4–5 is a later addition to vv 1–6.[14] Whether this was the case or not, one can envisage a storyteller opting to bypass vv 4–5 and complete his or her performance by linking 8:1–2 directly with 8:6. That is, at the end of the famine the woman returned and went directly to the king to demand the restoration of her house and land. At this point one may recall that when Elisha offered to speak to the king on her behalf in 4:13 she declined, stating that 'I live among my own people'. The implication is that she enjoyed direct access to the king, who was one of her people. According to 8:6, the king questioned the woman who presumably told him her story (a storyteller might choose to flesh out the meaning of the verb 'told' in v 6). He then appointed a eunuch (Hebrew *saris)* with instructions to see that all her property was restored to her.

However, the inclusion of 8:4–5 provides a valuable 'user base' for storytellers to link the distinct stories in the preceding chapters. It does so by bringing Elisha's servant Gehazi into the foreground. The king is portrayed seeking him out to recount 'all the great things that Elisha has done', and while Gehazi was telling him about the woman whose son Elisha raised from the dead, the woman herself entered the scene and was immediately identified by Gehazi as the one about whom he was telling the king. Gehazi is here depicted as the epitome of the loyal servant: he willingly proclaimed all the good that his master had done and did not hesitate to identify the woman as proof of the truth of his words and the prophetic status of his master. But the

---

14. *Cf* Mulzer, 'Der kranke und der gesunde Gehasi', 23; also Burke O Long, *2 Kings,* FOTL, X (Grand Rapids: Eerdmans, 1991), 98.

Gehazi portrayed in this scene is in marked contrast to the way he is depicted in the story of the healing of the leper Naaman in chapter 5. There Gehazi is exposed as a disloyal servant of the prophet; he lied to Naaman about what Elisha said (*cf* 5:22) and subsequently lied to Elisha about his encounter with Naaman (*cf* 5:25–26). For this he was struck with the leprosy of Naaman.

The text does not inform a reader how the lying and punished Gehazi of chapter 5 became once again the loyal servant of his master in 8:4–5. According to the theory of text as 'user base' this gap would have provided a storyteller with a creative opportunity. He or she could portray Gehazi repenting of his lies, accepting of his punishment, and recommitting himself to Elisha. His exchange with the king serves as a powerful sign of his transformation. A factor that a storyteller would need to take-into-account here is Gehazi's leprosy. According to 8:4–5 he was in the company of the king. A number of commentators have seen the leprosy factor as an indication of the artificial nature of the arrangement and that the textual sequence is not chronological; another view is that the redactor who made the link deliberately omitted any reference to Gehazi's leprosy in order to avoid the issue. A third view is that a reader is to presume Gehazi had been cured of his leprosy by the time of his encounter with the king. It was a sign that the liar had repented and been forgiven.[15] However, when one takes-into-account the story of Naaman in chapter 5, there is no need for such views. Naaman is described as a leper, nevertheless he was 'a great man and in high favor with his master', and was able to travel with an extensive entourage to Israel. One can therefore imagine a repentant Gehazi able to converse with the king even though he was still afflicted by leprosy. For a storyteller who takes this line, the focus of his/her version would be that the real transformation in Gehazi did not involve physical cure but a commitment to proclaim truthfully what Elisha said and did. This also provides a thematic link with the portrayal of the woman in 8:1–2. As she is portrayed faithfully obeying the prophetic word, so Gehazi is no longer a liar in the words he proclaims about Elisha to others such as the king. One could say that he was transformed into a faithful preacher of the good news about what the prophet said and did.

---

15. For a discussion of these proposals see Mulzer, 'Der kranke und der gesunde Gehasi', 19–27.

In light of these observations, we can now see how a storyteller could employ aspects of 8:1–6 to portray a similar transformation in the relationship between the king of Israel and Elisha. The king is mentioned in the story of Elisha and the woman of Shunem (*cf* 4:13), and in the story of Naaman the Aramean where the prophet came to his rescue after he interpreted the Aramean king's letter of introduction as a threat. But it is the subsequent stories of war between Israel and Aram in 6:8–7:20 that provide the best option for a storyteller to present a transformation in the relationship between Elisha and his king, and it is one that forms a fitting climax to the sequence of three relationships—between Elisha and the woman, between Elisha and Gehazi, and between Elisha and the king of Israel. There are two accounts of war between Aram and Israel in 6:8–7:20. In the first (*cf* 6:8–23), an attacking Aramean army was blinded by Yhwh in response to Elisha's prayer; he subsequently led them into the capital Samaria where he refused to allow the king to kill them and instead threw a party for them before sending them home. According to 6:24 a second war erupted some time later when king Ben-hadad of Aram laid siege to Samaria. The reaction of the king of Israel to the siege in 6:25–32 indicates that he blamed Elisha for it because he refused to allow the king to kill the Arameans during their earlier campaign. He vowed to kill the prophet but the latter has foreknowledge of this and was able to secure his safety.

When the king arrived on the scene Elisha prophesied the city's deliverance but did not mention any involvement of the king or his army, except to assert that although the king's doubting captain would see the restoration of the city's food supplies he would not get to eat of it (7:2). Yhwh subsequently dispersed the Aramean army in accord with the prophetic word, and their abandoned camp was discovered by four lepers. But when this was reported to the king of Israel, he refused to believe it was in accord with what Elisha prophesied and provided an alternative explanation that he declared to be the true one (*cf* 7:12). In effect he asserted the truth of his own words over those of the prophet. But events, as recounted in the text, proved him wrong, and the truth of Elisha's words was underscored by the abundance of food that suddenly became available to the people, and by the death of the king's captain at the gate. The king had appointed him to control movement in and out of the city and thereby assert royal authority. But he was trampled to death in the stampede to get to the food in the Aramean camp. In accord with Elisha's prophecy, he got to see food being brought into the city from the Aramean camp but did not get to eat of it. Was it this dramatic deliverance of the city that was in accord with Elisha's word but completely contrary to the king's word that led to the latter changing his attitude to the prophet? Given the way 8:1–6 portrays the king, it is reasonable to conclude that an ancient storyteller would have followed this line of development, or something like it.

On the basis of these reflections, one may discern the following connections between the portrayals of the three characters in 8:1–6. The woman of Shunem is portrayed as initially questioning—one may presume from the story in 4:3–37 in an honest way—the authenticity of the man whom she initially described as 'a man of God'. However, in light of Elisha restoring her son to life, she accepted his status as a prophet and the authority of his word. Hence, she unquestioningly obeyed his advice in 8:1–2 to seek refuge from the famine. Gehazi is not only portrayed in chapter 5 as a false or lying messenger of the prophetic word to Naaman but also as a lying servant of his master. However, according to 8:4–5 he was transformed into a messenger who faithfully proclaimed the 'good news' about what Elisha said and did. For his part the king of Israel is initially depicted in the war stories with Aram openly rejecting the prophetic word about the outcome of the war, and underscoring this by attempting to take control of the post-war situation on his terms (*cf* his appointment of the captain to oversee traffic through the gate of the city). According to 8:4–6 he sought out Gehazi to hear the 'good news' about all that Elisha said and did, a clear indication that he had come to accept the truth of Elisha's prophetic word. As well as this, v. 6 reports him appointing an official to ensure the restoration of all that belonged to the woman of Shunem before she fled the famine. Hence he acted on behalf of the other, of one of his subjects, and not for his own gain, as was the case in his disastrous appointment of the captain to have charge of the gate of the city.

This presentation of the meaning and function of 8:1–6 in relation to the preceding stories about the woman of Shunem, Gehazi, and the king of Israel, invites comment on their relationship to three encounters between Elisha and members of a group called the 'sons of the prophets' in 4:1–6, 38–44; and 6:1–7. Each encounter precedes one of the dramatic stories and each involves Elisha working a miracle in response to a plea for help. According to 4:1–6 Elisha's prophetic power enabled a widow to have sufficient oil to pay off her debts and avoid having her children become slaves of a creditor. According to 4:38–41 Elisha came to the aid of the 'sons of the prophets' during a famine by miraculously making a poisonous stew edible, and according to 4:42–44 he also made available a gift of food that a man from Baal-shalishah had brought to him as a gift. According to 6:1–7, Elisha miraculously retrieved an axe head from the Jordan so that one of the 'sons of the prophets' could continue building their new residence. A notable feature of these episodes is the contrast between the way the 'sons of the prophets' are depicted relying on and obeying Elisha, and their initial attitude to him in 2:15–18. Their proposal to search for Elijah indicates they were reluctant to accept Elisha as the new prophetic authority.

One can see how the change or transformation in the relationship between Elisha and the 'sons of the prophets' anticipates the more dramatic relationships between Elisha and the three characters in the stories.[16] They are more dramatic in that they involve not only the characters' relationships with the prophet but also with Yhwh. They are reported in 8:1–6 in a way that provides a storyteller with creative opportunities for development in oral performance. As a final comment, I would note that the subsequent text effects a kind of reversal in relation to the preceding miracle episodes. When the king of Israel (presumably Jehoram/Joram) reverts to the policies of his father Ahab, Elisha commands one of the 'sons of the prophets' to anoint Jehu king and thus bring-to-an-end the house of Ahab (cf 2 Kgs 9:1–10:36).[17] According to the preceding miracle episodes, the 'sons of the prophets' are those who by obeying Elisha's word resolve crises within their company. Now one them is called to obey Elisha's word and so resolve the crisis of kingship in Israel. Within the larger context, his anointing of Jehu fulfils Yhwh's command to Elijah in 1 Kings 19:16. The sequence provides creative and challenging opportunities for a storyteller.[18]

---

16. Heller thinks the 'sons of the prophets' are portrayed negatively ('petulant', 'helpless', 'childish', etc; cf *The Characters of Elijah and Elisha*, 189). However, I do not think he takes-into-account sufficiently the contrast between their behaviour in 2:15–18 and in the subsequent episodes.

17. Jehoram's recidivism parallels that of Ahab. The story of Naboth's vineyard in 1 Kgs 21 presents him as repentant when confronted by Elijah and forgiven by Yhwh, but according to 1 Kgs 22 he reverts to his former rebellious behaviour.

18. Readers may compare my analysis with that of Gilmour (*Juxtaposition and the Elisha Cycle*, 184–90), who initially reads 2 Kgs 8:1–6 independently, and then in relation to what precedes and follows.

Contributors

Brendan Byrne, SJ, Melbourne, is a lecturer in biblical studies at the University of Divinity, Melbourne and worked closely for many years at Jesuit Theological College, Melbourne.

Sarah Hart, lectures in biblical studies at Te Kupenga—Catholic Theological College, Auckland, New Zealand. Sarah was the last doctoral student of Tony Campbell.

Michael Kelly, SJ, is a Jesuit priest and started Jesuit Communications, publishers of Eureka Street and Australian Catholics, Church Resources which launched CathNews, a director of UCA News and is publisher of La Croix International and of the English edition of La Civilta Cattolica.

Mark O'Brien, OP, lectures in biblical studies at the University of Divinity, Melbourne and worked with Tony on a number of writing projects.

Nicole Rotaru, RSM, Melbourne, and was a close friend of Tony's for many years.

Bill Uren, SJ, Newman College, University of Melbourne, was a close friend of Tony's in the Jesuits.

ANTONY F. CANPBELL, SJ

Brief curriculum vitae

DEGREES

B.A. (Hons)	University of Melbourne	1964
M.A.	University of Melbourne	1972
S.T.L.	Faculty of Theology, Lyon-Fourvière	1968
L.S.S.	Pontifical Biblical Institute, Rome	1970
Ph.D.	Claremont Graduate School	1974
D.D.	Melbourne College of Divinity	1994 (earned senior degree)

POSITIONS

Professor of Old Testament, Jesuit Theological College	1974—
Dean, Jesuit Theological College	1975–85
President, Catholic Biblical Association of Australia	1975–76
Secretary, Fellowship for Biblical Studies	1975–93
Principal, Jesuit Theological College	1986–91
President, Fellowship for Biblical Studies	1990 and 2001

AWARDS

Fellow of the Society of Biblical Literature/Claremont Center for Biblical Research and Archives	1976–77

MEMBERSHIPS

Australian Association for the Study of Religion	1975–94
Australia and New Zealand Society for Theological Studies	1974–96
Australian Catholic Biblical Association	1974—
Catholic Biblical Association of America (life member)	1971—
Council of Christians and Jews (Victoria, Australia)	1985–96
Fellowship for Biblical Studies	1974—
Society of Biblical Literature	1974–2001

Fr Antony Campbell SJ was born and educated in New Zealand; in 1953 he moved to Australia to join the Jesuit Order. After philosophy, he studied classics and semitics in Melbourne, theology in France, scripture in Rome, and took his PhD in the Old Testament at Claremont Graduate School, California, in 1974. The DD, an earned senior degree, was awarded by the Melbourne College of Divinity in 1994.

Fr Campbell taugh Old Testament at Jesuit Theological College, within the ecumenical United Faculty of Theology, Parkville, in Melbourne, Australia. He has taught in graduate institutions in the USA, and has lectured widely in renewal courses and similar opportunities for presenting faith and the Older Testament to a wider public.

Bibliography

1964–1965 'Homer and Ugaritic Literature', in *Abr-Naharin*, 5:29–56.

1969 'Jeremiah's Use of the Covenant Formula', in *Lectures on the Covenant Formula given by Norbert Lolefink S.J.* (Polycopied presentation; Rome: Pontifical Biblical Institute).

1969 'An Historical Prologue in a Seventh-Century Treaty', in *Bib* 50: 534–45.

1975 *The Ark Narrative (1 Sam 4-6; 2 Sam 6): A Form-Critical and TraditioHistorical Study*, SBLDS, 16 (Missoula, MT: Scholars Press).

1976 'Bultmann and the Old Testament', in *Colloquium* 9: 34–36.

1979 'Psalm 78: A Contribution to the Theology of Tenth Century Israel', in *CBQ* 41: 51–79.

1979 'Yahweh and the Ark: A Case Study in Narrative', in *JBL* 98: 31–43.

1979 'The Yahwist Revisited', in *AusBR* 27: 2–14.

1980 'Our Changing Understanding of an Unchanging God', in *Word in Life* 28: 131–35.

1981–82 'The Old Testament and Women Today', in *Compass Theology Review* 15 . 4: 1–9.

1982 'God's Anger and Our Suffering', in *The Australasian Catholic Record* 59: 373–85.

1985 'A Paradigm for Language in Talking of the Spiritual and Psychological', in Edmond Chiu (ed.), Psychiatry and Religion: Proceedings of a Conference. 27–28th June 1985, St Vincent's Hospital Melbourne (Melbourne: St Vincent's Hospital): 132–38.

1986	'From Philistine to Throne (I Sam 16.14-18.16)', in AusBR 34: 35–41.
1986	*Of Prophets and Kings: A Late Ninth-Century Document (1 Samuel J-2 Kings 10)* CBQMS, I 7 (Washington: Catholic Biblical Association of America).
1987	'The Literary Approach to the Old Testament', in Erich Osborn and Lawrence McIntosh (eds), The Bible and European Literature: History and Hermeneutics (Melbourne: Melbourne Academic Press), 147–51.
1987	'Who Dares Wins: Reflections on the Story of David and Goliath and the Understanding of Human Freedom', in Edmond Chiu (ed), *The Psychological and Theological Meaning of Freedom: Proceeding of Second Conference. Psychiatry and Religion, 10th October, 1986* (Melbourne: St Vincent's Hospital), 59–66.
1988	'Job: Case Study or Theology', in Edmond Chiu (ed), *Psychiatry and Religion: Proceedings of Third Conference 23rd October, 1987* (Melbourne: St Vincent's Hospital), 38–44.
1989	'God Anger, and the Old Testament ', in Edmond Chiu (ed), *Psychiatry and Religion: Anger-A Psycho-Theological Analysis. Proceedings of Fourth Conference, 2nd September, 1988* (Melbourne: St Vincent's Hospital), 15–19.
1989	'Poverty and the Old Testament', in *Compass Theology Review* 23: 21–28.
1989	*The Study Companion to Old Testament Literature: An Approach to the Writings of Pre-Exilic and Exilic Israel*, Old Testament Studies, 2 (Wilmington, DE: Michael Glazier [republished in 1992 under the same title by Liturgical Press).
1989	'The Reported Story: Midway Between Oral Performance and Literary Art', in Semeia 46: 77–85.
1990	'God: Judge or Lover?', in *The Way* 30: 92–102.
1990	'1 Samuel', in RE Brown., JA Fitzmyer and RE Murphy (eds), *The New Jerome Biblical Commentary* (Englewood Cliffs, NJ: Prentice-Hall), 145–154.
1991	'Old Testament Narrative as Theology', in *Pacifica* 4: 165–80.
1991	'Past History and Present Text: The Clash of Classical and Post-Critical Approaches to Biblical Text', in *AusBR* 39: 1–18.

| 1993 | (with MA O'Brien) *Sources of the Pentateuch: Texts, Introductions, Annotations* (Minneapolis: Fortress Press). |

1993   'The Priestly Text: Redaction or Source', in G Braulik, W Gross and S McEvenue (eds), *Biblische Theologie und gesellschaftlicher Wandel: Fiir Norbert Lolefink SJ* (Freiburg: Herder), 32–47.

1994   'Martin Noth and the Deuteronomistic History', in SL McKenzie and MP Graham (eds), *The History of Israel's Traditions: The Heritage of Martin Noth,* JSOTSup, 182 (Sheffield: Sheffield Academic Press), 31–62.

1996   *The Authority of Scripture: Canon as Invitation* (Claremont, CA: Institute for Antiquity and Christianity).

1997   'Structure Analysis and the Art of Exegesis (1 Samuel 16.14-18.30)', in Henry TC Sun *et al* (eds), *Problems in Biblical Theology: Essays in Honor of Rolf Knierim* (Grand Rapids: Eerdmans), 76–103.

1998   (with MA O'Brien) '1–2 Samuel', in WR Farmer *et al* (eds), *The International Bible Commentary* (Collegeville, MN: Liturgical Press), 572–607.

1998   (with MA O'Brien) '1–2 Kings', in WR Farmer *et al* (eds), *The international Bible Commentary* (Collegeville, MN: Liturgical Press), 608–643.

2000   *God First Loved Us: The Challenge of Accepting Unconditional Love* (New York/Mahwah, NJ: Paulist Press).

2000   (with M.A. O'Brien) *Unfolding the Deuteronomistic History: Origins, Upgrades, Present Text* (Minneapolis: Fortress Press).

2000   'Women Storytellers in Ancient Israel', in *AusBR* 48: 72–73.

2001   'Preparatory Issues in Approaching Biblical Texts', in Leo G Perdue (ed), *The Blackwell Companion to the Hebrew Bible* (Oxford: Basil Blackwell), 3–18.

2002   'Invitation or . . . ?: The Bible's Role', in *AusBR* 50: 1–9.

2002   'The Storyteller's Role: Reported Story and Biblical Text', in *CBQ* 64: 427–441.

2003   *1 Samuel,* FOTL, 7 (Grand Rapids: Eerdmans).

2003   'Form Criticism's Future', in Marvin A. Sweeney and Ehud Ben Zvi (eds), *The Changing Face of Form Criticism for the Twenty-First Century* (Grand Rapids: Eerdmans), 15–31.

2003	'The Book of Job: Two Questions, One Answer', in *AusBR* 51: 15–25.
2004	'Ignatius Loyola and the Unconditional Love of God', in *The Way* 53.1: 31–42.
2004	*Joshua to Chronicles: An Introduction* (Louisville, KY: Westminster/John Knox Press).
2004	*2 Samuel*, FOTL, 8 (Grand Rapids: Eerdmans).
2005	(with MA O'Brien) *Rethinking the Pentateuch* (Louisville, KY: Westminster/ John Knox Press).
2010	*Making Sense of the Bible: Difficult Texts and Modern Faith* (New York. Mahwah, NJ: Paulist Press).
2012	*Experiencing Scripture: Intimacy with Ancient Text and Modern Faith* (Adelaide: ATF Press).
2013	'Pentateuch Beyond Sources; A New Paradigm', in *AUSBR*, 61: 18–29.
2014	*Opening the Bible: Selection of Writings of Antony F Campbell SJ* (Adelaide: ATF Press).
2018	'God and Suffering—'it happens': Job's Silent Solution', in *American Theological Enquiry* 3/1: 153–63.
2018	*Genesis Beyond Sources: A New Approach* (Adelaide: ATF Press).
2021	'2 Samuel', in *The Jerome Biblical Commentary for the Twenty First Century. Third Fully Revised Edition with a Foreword by Pope Francis* (London: T&T Clark Biblical Studies, Bloomsbury)

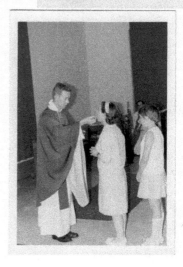

CPSIA information can be obtained
at www.ICGtesting.com
Printed in the USA
JSHW020806290322
24361JS00003B/255

9 781922 737212